AF782537

American Iron and Steel Institute

Steel Manufacturers Association

Specialty Steel Industry of North America

CPTI
The Committee on Pipe and Tube Imports

United Steelworkers of America

March 13, 2006

Honorable Harold Rogers
Chairman, House Committee on Appropriations
Homeland Security Subcommittee
U.S. House of Representatives
B-307 Rayburn House Office Building
Washington, DC 20515-6028

Honorable Martin Olav Sabo
Ranking Minority Member, House Committee on Appropriations,
Homeland Security Subcommittee
U.S. House of Representatives
1016 Longworth House Office Building
Washington, DC 20515

Dear Chairman and Ranking Minority Member:

We are submitting for your review a request endorsed by the American Iron and Steel Institute (AISI), Steel Manufacturers Association (SMA), Specialty Steel Industry of North America (SSINA), Committee on Pipe and Tube Imports (CPTI) and the United Steelworkers of America (USWA) for FY 07 funding to continue the 40-year liaison partnership between the U.S. steel industry and the Bureau of Customs and Border Protection (CBP).

This program, which has been government supported and funded since FY 03, is vital to CBP as it continues its commitment to strong commercial enforcement of the trade laws and the collection of duties on imports which have injured the industry and its workers. The presence of a growing global steel industry, with China at the forefront, will continue to present import challenges for the domestic steel industry and the use and enforcement of the trade laws is essential for the industry's ability to challenge unfair trade activities. Further, as the Department of Homeland Security continues to hold security and anti-terrorism as its number one priority, it is even more important for CBP officials engaged in commercial enforcement to have all the tools that are available to properly and more efficiently carry out their jobs. The Customs/Steel Partnership Program provides these tools.

The steel industry's highly successful partnership program with CBP, in continuous operation since the mid-1960s, has evolved into today's structure of regional seminars as well as various meetings at Customs Headquarters (HQ). Seminars provide an opportunity for Customs officials to receive first hand information from industry leaders on the technical aspects of steel customs issues that address an array of steel products. In addition, the seminars are also open to the import broker community and provide these professionals with valuable information on Customs rules, regulations and procedures at the nation's leading ports.

The program, tailored to meet the specific needs of the CBP, is well organized and managed by AISI. Industry participation is broad and comprehensive, consisting of members of AISI, some of whom are also members of SMA, as well as SSINA and CPTI. Costs to run the program in FY 07 are estimated at $500,000. This cost is equal to the appropriation for FY 06 and therefore does not reflect an increase in the program. The industry is confident and committed it can continue to deliver the program at the current FY 06 funding level.

Our industry team is comprised of commercial, legal and technical experts who highly value the opportunities afforded to them by the program to update CBP on all relevant enforcement issues in the dynamic arena of steel trade. This program has provided immeasurable benefits to our industry and to the Customs community and it has proven to be a successful partnership. We hope that Congress will support this request to continue this beneficial educational and enforcement program.

Thank you for your thoughtful consideration of our request. We look forward to working with you.

Sincerely,

Andrew G. Sharkey
President and CEO
American Iron and Steel Institute (AISI)

Thomas A. Danjczek
President
Steel Manufacturers Association (SMA)

Laurence J. Lasoff
Counsel
Specialty Steel Industry of North America (SSINA)

Roger B. Schagrin
Executive Director and General Counsel
Committee on Pipe and Tube Imports (CPTI)

William J. Klinefelter
Legislative and Political Director
United Steelworkers of America (USWA)

Cc:
Ben Nicholson, Office of Chairman Rogers
Jeff Ashford, Office of Chairman Rogers
Beverly Pheto, Office of Ranking Minority Member Sabo

Attachments

TESTIMONY OF

WILLIAM W. MILLAR, PRESIDENT

AMERICAN PUBLIC TRANSPORTATION ASSOCIATION

BEFORE THE

SUBCOMMITTEE ON HOMELAND SECURITY

OF THE

HOUSE COMMITTEE ON APPROPRIATIONS

****

March 16, 2006

SUBMITTED BY

American Public Transportation Association
1666 K Street, N.W.
Washington, DC 20006
Tel: (202) 496-4800
Fax: (202) 496-4324

APTA

APTA is a nonprofit international association of over 1,600 public and private member organizations including transit systems and commuter rail operators; planning, design, construction and finance firms; product and service providers; academic institutions; transit associations and state departments of transportation. APTA members serve the public interest by providing safe, efficient and economical transit services and products. Over ninety percent of persons using public transportation in the United States and Canada are served by APTA members.

Mr. Chairman, thank you for this opportunity to submit written testimony on the security and safety of public transportation systems. We appreciate your interest in transportation security, and we look forward to working with you as you develop the FY 2007 appropriations bill for the Department of Homeland Security.

ABOUT APTA

The American Public Transportation Association (APTA) is a nonprofit international association of more than 1,600 public and private member organizations including transit systems and commuter rail operators; planning, design, construction, and finance firms; product and service providers; academic institutions; transit associations and state departments of transportation. APTA members serve the public interest by providing safe, efficient, and economical transit services and products. More than ninety percent of the people using public transportation in the United States and Canada are served by APTA member systems.

OVERVIEW

Mr. Chairman, public transportation is one of our nation's critical infrastructures. We cannot overemphasize the critical importance of our industry to the economic quality of life of this country. Over 9.6 billion transit trips are taken annually on all modes of transit service. People use public transportation vehicles over 32 million times each weekday. This is more than sixteen times the number of daily travelers on the nation's airlines.

Safety and security are the top priority of the public transportation industry. Transit systems took many steps to improve security prior to 9/11 and have significantly increased efforts since then. Since September 11, 2001, public transit agencies in the United States have spent over $2 billion on security and emergency preparedness programs and technology from their own budgets with only minimal federal funding. Last year's events in London and the previous year's events in Madrid further highlight the need to strengthen security on public transit systems and to do so without delay. We do not need another wakeup call like the terrorists attacks on rail systems in London and Madrid.

We urge Congress to act decisively on this issue. In light of the documented needs, we respectfully urge Congress to provide at least $560 million in the FY 2007 Homeland Security Appropriations bill for transit security grants to assist transit systems to continue to address the $6 billion in identified transit security investment needs. Funding at this level annually would allow for dramatic improvement in security for the nation's transit users over a 10 year period. Federal funding for additional security needs should provide for both hard and soft costs as described below and will be in addition to investments as transit systems continue to provide from their own resources. We also respectfully urge Congress to provide $500,000 to the Department of Homeland Security (DHS) so that DHS can in turn provide that amount in grant funding to the APTA security standards program which includes participation with our federal partners to assist with the development of transit security standards. In addition, we respectfully urge Congress to provide $600,000 to maintain the Public Transit Information Sharing Analysis Center (ISAC).

BACKGROUND

In 2004 APTA surveyed its U.S. transit system members to determine what actions they needed to take to improve security for their customers, employees and facilities. In response to the survey, transit agencies around the country have identified in excess of $6 billion in transit security investment needs. State and local governments and transit agencies are doing what they can to improve security, but it is important that the federal government be a full partner in the effort to ensure the security of the nation's transit users.

In FY 2003, transit security was allocated $65 million in federal funds from DHS for 20 transit systems. In FY 2004, $50 million was allocated from DHS for 30 transit systems. For the first time in FY 2005, Congress specifically appropriated $150 million for transit, passenger and freight rail security. Out of the $150 million, transit is to receive approximately $130 million—almost $108 million for rail transit and more than $22 million for bus. Also, passenger ferries are slated to receive an additional $5 million for security from a separate account. In FY 2006, Congress appropriated $150 million for transit, passenger and freight rail security. DHS is currently deciding how to allocate this funding among the modes of transportation. We are very appreciative of this effort. However, in the face of significant needs, more needs to be done.

Transit authorities have significant and specific transit security needs. Based on APTA's 2003 Infrastructure Database survey, over 2,000 rail stations do not have security cameras. According to our 2005 Transit Vehicle Database, 53,000 buses, over 5,000 commuter rail cars, and over 10,000 heavy rail cars do not have security cameras. Fewer than one-half of all buses have automatic vehicle locator systems (AVLs) that allow dispatchers to know the location of the bus when an emergency occurs. Nearly 75 percent of demand response vehicles lack these AVLs. Furthermore, no transit system has a permanent biological detection system. In addition, only two transit authorities have a permanent chemical detection system. A partnership with the federal government could help to better address many of these specific needs.

We are disappointed that the Administration proposed only $600 million for a Targeted Infrastructure Protection Program in the FY 2007 DHS budget proposal, which would fund infrastructure security grants for transit, seaports, railways and other facilities. We are also disappointed that the Administration did not include a specific line item funding amount for transit security. We look forward to working with the Administration and Congress in securing adequate transit security funding that begins to address unmet transit security needs throughout the country.

We further request that the existing process for distributing DHS federal grant funding be modified so that funds are distributed directly to transit authorities, rather than to State Administrating Agencies (SAA) on a regional basis. We believe direct funding to the transit authorities would be more efficient and productive. The Administration's process and conditions that have been put into effect have created significant barriers and time delays in getting the actual funds into the hands of transit agencies.

As I noted in previous testimony, APTA is a Standards Development Organization (SDO) for the public transportation industry. We are now applying our growing expertise in standards development to transit industry safety and security, best practices, guidelines and standards as well. We have already begun to initiate our efforts for security standards development and we have engaged our federal partners from both the DHS and Department of Transportation in this process. Through these initial meetings, I am pleased to advise that our federal partners have agreed to support these efforts. We look forward to working with the Administration and Congress in support of this initiative. We respectfully urge Congress to provide $500,000 to the DHS so that it can in turn provide that amount in grant funding to the APTA security standards program which includes participation of our federal partners to assist with the development of such standards and practices consistent with what we have already seen through the Federal Transit Administration (FTA). Our efforts in standards development for commuter rail, rail transit and bus transit operations have been significant and our status as a SDO is acknowledged by both the FTA and the Federal Railroad Administration (FRA). The FTA and the Transportation Research Board have supported our standards initiatives through the provision of grants.

We also would like to work with Congress and the Department of Homeland Security's Directorate of Science and Technology to take a leadership role in advancing research and technology development to enhance security and emergency preparedness for public transportation.

INFORMATION SHARING

Since the terrorist attacks of September 11, 2001, public transit systems across the country have worked very hard to strengthen their security plans and procedures and have been very active in training personnel and conducting drills to test their capacity to respond to emergencies. As well, to the extent possible within their respective budgets, transit systems have been incrementally hardening their services through the introduction of additional technologies such as surveillance equipment, access control and intrusion detection systems. While the transit systems have been diligent, they have been unable to fully implement programs without more assistance from the federal government.

A vital component of ensuring public transit's ability to prepare and respond to critical events is the timely receipt of security intelligence in the form of threats, warnings, advisories and access to informational resources. Accordingly, in 2003, the American Public Transportation Association, supported by Presidential Decision Directive #63, established an ISAC for public transit systems throughout the United States. A funding grant in the amount of $1.2 million was provided to APTA by the Federal Transit Administration to establish a very successful Public Transit ISAC that operated 24 hours a day, 7 days a week, and gathered information from various sources, including DHS, and then passed information on to transit systems following a careful analysis of that information. However, given that the Federal Transit Administration was subsequently unable to access security funds, and given the decision of DHS to not fund ISAC operations, APTA then had to look for an alternate method of providing security intelligence through DHS's newly created Homeland Security Information Network (HSIN). APTA continues to work with DHS staff to create a useful HSIN application for the transit industry. It is clear, however, that while the HSIN may become an effective resource, it does not match the 24/7 two-way communication functions provided through the Public Transit ISAC. However, we believe that consistent, on-going and reliable funds from Congress should be provided for the Public Transit ISAC that has been proven an effective delivery mechanism for security intelligence. Therefore, we respectfully urge Congress to provide $600,000 to maintain the Public Transit ISAC.

In addition, APTA's membership includes many major international public transportation systems, including the London Underground, Madrid Metro, and the Moscow Metro. APTA also has a strong partnership with the European-based transportation association, the International Union of Public Transport. Through these relationships, APTA has participated in a number of special forums in Europe and Asia to give US transit agencies the benefit of their experiences and to help address transit security both here and abroad.

COST OF HEIGHTENED SECURITY

Following the attacks on London, APTA was asked to assist the TSA in conducting a teleconference between the TSA and transit officials to discuss transit impacts pertaining to both increasing and decreasing the DHS threat levels. There is no question that increased threat levels have a dramatic impact on budget expenditures of transit systems and extended periods pose significant impacts on personnel costs. These costs totaled $900,000 **per day** for US public transit systems or an estimated $33.3 million from July 7 to August 12, 2005 during the heightened state of "orange" for public transportation. This amount does not include costs associated with additional efforts by New York, New Jersey and other systems to conduct random searches.

Many transit systems are also implementing other major programs to upgrade security. For example, New York's Metropolitan Transportation Authority (NY-MTA) is taking broad and sweeping steps to help ensure the safety and security of its transportation systems in what are among the most extensive security measures taken by a public transportation system to date. NY-MTA will add 1,000 surveillance cameras and 3,000 motion sensors to its network of subways and commuter rail facilities as part of a $212 million security upgrade announced late last year with the Lockheed Martin Corporation. In fact, NY-MTA plans to spend over $1.1 billion between now and 2009 on transit security.

SECURITY INVESTMENT NEEDS

Mr. Chairman, since the awful events of 9/11, the transit industry has invested some $2 billion of its own funds for enhanced security measures, building on the industry's already considerable efforts. At the same time, our industry undertook a comprehensive review to determine how we could build upon our existing industry security practices. This included a range of activities, which include research, best practices, education, information sharing in the industry, and surveys. As a result of these efforts we have a better understanding of how to create a more secure environment for our riders and the most critical security investment needs.

Our latest survey of public transportation security identified enhancements of at least $5.2 billion in additional capital funding to maintain, modernize, and expand transit system security functions to meet increased security demands. Over $800 million in increased costs for security personnel, training, technical support, and research and development have been identified, bringing total additional transit security funding needs to more than $6 billion.

Responding transit agencies were asked to prioritize the uses for which they required additional federal investment for security improvements. Priority examples of operational improvements include:

Funding current and additional transit agency and local law enforcement personnel
Funding for over-time costs and extra security personnel during heightened alert levels
Training for security personnel
Joint transit/law enforcement training
Security planning activities
Security training for other transit personnel

Priority examples of security capital investment improvements include:

Radio communications systems
Security cameras on-board transit vehicles and in transit stations
Controlling access to transit facilities and secure areas
Automated vehicle locator systems
Security fencing around facilities

Transit agencies with large rail operations also reported a priority need for federal capital funding for intrusion detection devices.

Mr. Chairman, the Department of Homeland Security issued directives for the transit industry in May 2004 which would require that transit authorities beef up security and to take a series of precautions which would set the stage for more extensive measures without any federal funding assistance. Transit systems have already carried out many of the measures that Transportation Security Administration (TSA) is calling for, such as drafting security plans, removing trash bins and setting up procedures to deal with suspicious packages. The cost of these measures and further diligence taken during times of heightened alert is of particular concern to us. We look forward to working with you in addressing these issues.

As you know, in the FY 2006 Homeland Security Appropriations bill (PL 109-90), TSA can hire rail inspectors using an $8 million appropriation. We have concerns about this provision. We believe that funding for the inspectors would be better spent on things that would support the industry such as surveillance cameras, emergency communication and other systems rather than highlighting security issues without providing the necessary resources to address them. We look forward to working with you in addressing our concerns.

ONGOING TRANSIT SECURITY PROGRAMS

Mr. Chairman, while transit agencies have moved to a heightened level of security alertness, the leadership of APTA has been actively working with its strategic partners to develop a practical plan to address our industry's security and emergency preparedness needs. In light of our new realities for security, the APTA Executive Committee has established a Security Affairs Steering Committee. This committee addresses our security strategic issues and directions for our initiatives. This committee will also serve as the mass transit sector coordination council that will interface with DHS and other federal agencies forming the government coordinating council.

In partnerships with the Transportation Research Board, APTA supported two TCRP Panels that identified and initiated specific projects developed to address *Preparedness/Detection/Response to Incidents* and *Prevention and Mitigation.*

In addition to the TCRP funded efforts, APTA has been instrumental in the development of numerous security and emergency preparedness tools and resources. Many of these resources were developed in close partnership with the FTA and we are presently focused on continuing that same level of partnership with various entities within DHS. Also, APTA has reached out to other organizations and international transportation associations to formally engage in sharing information on our respective security programs and to continue efforts that raise the bar for safety and security effectiveness.

APTA has long-established safety audit programs for commuter rail, bus, and rail transit operations. Within the scope of these programs are specific elements pertaining to *Emergency Response Planning and Training* as well as *Security Planning.* In keeping with our industry's increased emphasis on these areas, the APTA Safety Management Audit Programs have been modified to place added attention to these critical elements.

CONCLUSION

Mr. Chairman, in light of our nation's heightened security needs post 9/11, we believe that increased federal investment in public transportation security by Congress and DHS is critical. The public transportation industry has made great strides in transit security improvements since 9/11 but much more needs to be done. Therefore, we respectfully urge Congress to provide at least $560 million in the FY 2007 Department of Homeland Security Appropriations bill for transit security grants to assist transit systems to continue to address the $6 billion in identified transit security investment needs. Funding at this level annually would also allow for dramatic improvement in security for the nation's transit users over a 10 year period. We also respectfully urge Congress to provide $500,000 to the Department of Homeland Security so that DHS can in turn provide that amount in grant funding to the APTA security standards program which includes participation of our federal partners to assist with the development of transit security standards and practices consistent with what we have already seen through the FTA. In addition, we respectfully urge Congress to provide $600,000 to maintain the Public Transit ISAC.

We have also found that investment in public transit security programs, resources and infrastructures provides a direct benefit in preparation and response to natural disasters as well. We look forward to building on our cooperative working relationship with the Department of Homeland Security and Congress to begin to address these needs. We again thank you and the Committee for allowing us to submit testimony on these critical issues and look forward to working with you on safety and security issues.

BRUCE BAUGHMAN
PRESIDENT, NATIONAL EMERGENCY MANAGEMENT ASSOCIATION
AND DIRECTOR, ALABAMA EMERGENCY MANAGEMENT AGENCY

STATEMENT FOR THE RECORD

APPROPRIATIONS FOR THE DEPARTMENT OF HOMELAND SECURITY FOR FISCAL YEAR 2007

THE UNITED STATES HOUSE REPRESENTATIONS
APPROPRIATIONS SUBCOMMITTEE ON HOMELAND SECURITY

MARCH 16, 2006

INTRODUCTION
Thank you Chairman Rogers, Ranking Member Sabo, and distinguished members of the Committee for allowing me the opportunity to provide you with a statement for the record on the Department of Homeland Security (DHS) fiscal year 2007 budget. I am Bruce Baughman, the President of the National Emergency Management Association and Director of the Alabama Emergency Management Agency. In my statement, I am representing the National Emergency Management Association (NEMA), whose members are the state emergency management directors in the states, the U.S. territories, and the District of Columbia. NEMA's members are responsible to their governors for emergency preparedness, homeland security, mitigation, response, and recovery activities for natural, man-made, and terrorist caused disasters.

As you consider the budget for FY 2007, emergency management in our country has received greater attention as a result of the aftermath of Hurricane Katrina. However, funding has not followed from the federal government to assist in meeting the needs for all-hazards emergency preparedness, response, recovery, and mitigation activities. Over the past year, our nation's emergency management system has been tested by the extensive natural disasters that we have faced. In all, there were 48 major disaster declarations, 68 emergency declarations, and 39 fire management assistance declarations. Every single state was impacted by one of these declarations, including the District of Columbia, and all but two of the U.S. territories. Forty-eight states were impacted enough by Hurricanes Katrina and Rita to warrant declarations for federal assistance, whether the states were disaster areas or the states received significant numbers of evacuees. States have been mandated under stringent timeframes to complete comprehensive reviews of evacuation plans and other emergency plans with no federal support. At the same time, emergency management continues to prepare for the threat of terrorism with numerous other requirements mandated by the federal government such as updating state plans to reflect the National Response Plan (NRP), training emergency responders and state and local officials on the National Incident Management System (NIMS), and implementing the National Preparedness Goal mandated by Homeland Security Presidential Directive 8 (HSPD 8) on National Preparedness **with no additional federal financial assistance to meet federal mandates.** The multi-hazards emergency management system continues to be the means to practice and exercise for devastating acts of terrorism, while at the same time preparing the nation for hurricanes, tornadoes, hazardous materials spills, and floods. We respectfully ask for your Committee to consider the role of emergency management as you address the FY 2007 appropriations and ask for your serious consideration of federal support for the Emergency Management Performance Grant Program (EMPG) to build state and local emergency management capacity.

The Department of Homeland Security budget provides critical support to state and local emergency management programs. NEMA would like to address three critical issues regarding the proposed federal budget for Department of Homeland Security:

1. **Extreme concern for proposed cuts to the Emergency Management Performance Grant (EMPG) program while requirements increase for state and local governments;**
2. **The need for federal support for the Emergency Management Assistance Compact (EMAC); and**
3. **Concerns related to the status of reorganizations at the Department of Homeland Security.**

EMERGENCY MANAGEMENT INFRASTRUCTURE FUNDING
EMPG is the only program for All-Hazards Preparedness/Readiness

Natural disasters are certain and often anticipated. Every state must be able to plan for disasters as well as build and sustain the capability to respond. EMPG is the only source of funding to assist state and local governments with planning and preparedness/readiness activities associated with natural disasters. At a time when our country is recovering from one of the largest natural disasters in history and making strides to improve the nation's emergency preparedness/readiness, we cannot afford to have this vital program be cut by $13.1 million. EMPG is the backbone of the nation's all-hazards emergency management system and the only source of direct federal funding to state and local governments for emergency management capacity building. EMPG is used for personnel, planning, training, and exercises at both the state and local levels. EMPG is primarily used to support state and local emergency management personnel who are responsible for writing plans, conducting training, exercises and corrective action, educating the public on disaster readiness and maintaining the nation's emergency response system. EMPG is being used to help states create and update plans for receiving and distribution plans for commodities and ice after a disaster, debris removal plans, and plans for receiving or evacuating people – all of these critical issues identified in the aftermath of Hurricane Katrina.

The state and local government partnership with the federal government to ensure preparedness dates back to the civil defense era of the 1950s, yet increased responsibilities over the last decade have fallen on state and local governments. NEMA completed a Quick Response Survey in March 2006 to assess the impacts of the proposed cut to the EMPG program. Of the 42 states responding, 90 percent of the states will have to cut staff ranging from one person to more than 50 positions. If the cut is included in the budget: 20 states will have to cut between 1-10 positions; 10 states will have to cut between 11-30 positions; 4 will have to cut between 31-50 positions; and 4 will have to cut more than 50 positions. In the same Quick Response Survey, 83 percent of responding states report that the majority of EMPG funds go to local grants, so the impact of the cut would be greatest on local governments.

State and Local Match

EMPG is the only program in the Preparedness Account within the Department of Homeland Security that requires a match at the state and local level. The match is evidence of the commitment by state and local governments to address the urgent need for all- hazards emergency planning, to include terrorism. EMPG requires a match of 50 percent from the state or local governments. According to the NEMA 2004 Biennial Report, budgets for state emergency management agencies nationally were reduced by an average of 23 percent in fiscal year 2004, yet at the same time states were continuing to over match the federal government's commitment to national security protection through EMPG by $96 million in FY04, which is a 80 percent state and 20 percent federal contribution.

EMPG Helps Ensure Personnel for Mutual Aid

During last year's hurricane season, the interdependencies of the nation's emergency management system were demonstrated and one of the success stories was the Emergency Management Assistance Compact (EMAC). EMAC enabled 48 states, the District of Columbia, the Virgin Islands, and Puerto Rico to provide assistance in the form of more than 2100 missions of human, military and equipment assets and over 65,00 civilian and military personnel and equipment assets to support the impacted states. The estimated costs of these missions may exceed $829 million and the missions and requests for aid are continuing. Of the personnel providing assistance through EMAC, 46,448 were National Guard personnel and 19,431 were civilians. Many of the civilians sent to provide assistance were supported by the EMPG program. The nature of the nation's mutual aid system vividly shows the need for all states to have appropriate capabilities to respond to disasters of all types and sizes. EMPG allows states and local governments to build this capacity both for their own use and to share in through EMAC. The increased reliance on mutual aid due to catastrophic disasters means additional resources are needed to continue to build and enhance the nation's mutual aid system through EMAC.

Appropriate Support Needed to Strengthen Program

While EMPG received modest increases in 2003 and 2004 after ten years of straight-lined funding, the program still needs significant investment to accomplish its goals. The final FY 2006 DHS conference report provided an additional $5 million for the program. After the across the board cut, the program was left with $183.1 million. We appreciate all of the efforts of members of Congress and the Administration to allow for these increases. Continued funding increases are necessary to make up for a decade of degradation of funding and increased state and local commitments because funding has not kept pace with inflation or with increasing demand. The increased flexibility of EMPG is offset by funding shortfalls estimated in the NEMA Biennial Report in 2004 to be over $264 million for all 50 states. The current shortfall is $260, because of the $3.1 million increase in FY 2006.

The President's budget proposal will have a devastating impact on the nation's emergency management system at the same time that responsibilities are increasing for new and emerging hazards. The proposal decreases funding for the EMPG program by $10 million. Congress affirmed the intent of the program as all-hazards and dedicated to supporting personnel during consideration of the FY 2006 budget. NEMA is appreciative of Congress' recognition of the EMPG program, but this year we respectfully ask that Congress aggressively address the programs shortfalls with an additional $87 million in funding for EMPG for FY 2007, for a total of $270 million.

Clearly, Congress wants to understand what is being built with these investments, especially in tight fiscal conditions. The 2006 Quick Response Survey found that if states were to each receive an additional $1 million in EMPG funding for FY 2007, states would use the following percentages for the following activities: 88 percent of states responding would use the funding to support the update plans including evacuation, sheltering, emergency operations, catastrophic disasters and others; 83 percent would provide more training opportunities for state and local emergency preparedness and response; 88 percent would provide additional preparedness grants to local jurisdictions; 69 percent would conduct more state and local exercises; and 61 percent would use funding for state and local NIMS compliance.

Accountability Measures

Many states have various accountability measures in place to track the use of EMPG funding and NEMA supports the development of a national system that quantifies the uses of the funding. In fact, NEMA through the National Homeland Security Consortium is working closely with the new Preparedness Directorate at DHS to work collaborate on performance metrics for HSPD-8 and the Target Capabilities List. The DHS effort will help to develop a national picture of EMPG metrics as well. At the same time, states already have measures in place at the state level to track the use of EMPG funding in their states. Some of the measures in place reported in the 2006 Quick Response Survey include: 95 percent of responding states have reporting requirements ; 76 percent of states responding require the development of state-wide goals that must be met with the funds; 61 percent of the states responding call for local governments to demonstrate performance against goals that are written by local jurisdictions; 42 percent of responding states implement corrective action plans if goals are not met with funding; and 45 percent of states tie program funding to meeting the standards in place with the voluntary Emergency Management Accreditation Program (EMAP) for state and local emergency management agencies.

EMPG as a Separate Account

The President's Budget proposal for FY 2007 suggests combining the EMPG account with the Citizen Corp account to form a formula-based grant account. NEMA strongly disagrees with this approach, as EMPG must be maintained as a separate line item account as Congress has affirmed since FY 2003. Congress agreed at that time that the program account needed to be visible and easy to find in the budget because of the importance of the program. The separate account is critical because the program is the only all-hazards grant program being administered through the Grants and Training Office to emergency management agencies. Additionally, we suggest that Congress maintain the method of distribution for EMPG, similar to the language in the FY 2006 appropriations, however continuing to allocate the funding through the State Administrative Agencies (SAAs) continues to cause delays in some states. NEMA supports language that would expressly restore the direct allocation and administration of the EMPG grants to state emergency management agencies. This will facilitate the process of expediting funding to state and local emergency management agencies.

All-Hazards Approach

The federal government must continue its commitment to ensuring national security though all-hazard preparedness. Without adequate numbers of state and local personnel to operate the all-hazards emergency management system, the infrastructure used to prevent, prepare for, respond to, and recover from all disasters will collapse. Unfortunately, Hurricanes Katrina and Rita illustrated the need for adequate emergency management systems from the ground up. Instead of making unbalanced investments towards terrorism preparedness, we must maintain an all-hazards approach and shore up the foundation of our response system for all disasters regardless of cause. We strongly ask for Congress to ensure predictable and adequate funding levels for the EMPG in FY 2007.

BUIDING OUR NATION'S MUTUAL AID SYSTEM THROUGH EMAC

The response to Hurricanes Katrina and Rita resulted in the largest deployment of interstate mutual aid in the nation's history through the Emergency Management Assistance Compact (EMAC). As mentioned previously, EMAC deployed personnel comprised of multiple disciplines from all member states to respond to Louisiana, Mississippi, Alabama, Florida, and Texas. EMAC Operations in Louisiana are still underway. The process enabled National Guard, search and rescue teams, incident management teams, emergency operations center support, building inspectors, and law enforcement personnel to immediately assist the requesting states in need of support. The National Guard even chose to continue under EMAC when deployed under Title 32 because of the organization, liability protections, accountability, and tracking abilities EMAC provides.

EMAC was created after Hurricane Andrew by then-Florida Governor Lawton Chiles. The system was developed through the members states of the Southern Governors' Association to establish mechanisms to enable mutual aid among member sates in emergency situations. The Southern Regional Emergency Management Assistance Compact (SREMAC) was signed by participating Governors in 1993. Following recognition of SREMACs nationwide applicability by the National Governors' Association and FEMA, Congress enacted EMAC in 1996 (P.L. 104-321). Currently 49 states, the U.S. Virgin Islands, Puerto Rico, and the District of Columbia are members of EMAC. Hawaii is currently considering legislation to become a party to the compact during their current legislative session. EMAC requires member states to have an implementation plan and to follow procedures outlined in the EMAC Operations Manual. EMAC takes care of issues such as reimbursement, liability protections, and workers' compensation issues.

Prior to the historic 2005 deployments, EMAC's largest previous deployment was during the 2004 Hurricane season in Florida, Alabama, and West Virginia, which enabled 38 states to provide assistance in the form of more than $15 million in human, military, and equipment assets and over 800 personnel to support the impacted states for over 85 days of continuous response operations. NEMA utilized the grant funds to work with an independent consulting company to complete a 2004 After Action Report, that identified areas for continuous improvement for the EMAC systems and EMAC has worked to draft a strategic plan to implement the lessons learned into practice. NEMA is currently working to complete an After-Action Report on the 2005 hurricane season, with a meeting of stakeholders, assisting states, requesting states, and others later this month. The report is expected to be complete by September 2006 and the strategic plan will be amended to reflect new lessons learned. The support of EMAC is critical to helping offset the costs of disasters and maintaining the need for a massive federal workforce for response to catastrophic disasters. The beauty of EMAC is that it provides assistance to those in need, but allows others to assist and learn from disasters in other states.

In order to meet the ever-growing need for and reliance on interstate mutual aid, EMAC is seeking $4 million over three years to continue to build EMAC capabilities. This funding will allow EMAC to focus on the implementation of lessons learned from Hurricanes Katrina and Rita such as training and education for all mutual aid stakeholders, resource typing and credentialing, and information and resource management. Since EMAC's inception in 1993, EMAC was funded by member states until 2003. In 2003, FEMA funded EMAC with a 3 year grant of $2 million. This funding expires in November 2006. Funding has been used for administrative support of EMAC, development of the EMAC Operations system whereby all resources deployed under the Compact are tracked from when it is requested until reimbursement is paid, and the 2004 and 2005 after action reports.

SECOND STAGE REVIEW AND FEMA

As the Congress looks at the lessons learned and recommendations for reform included in reports following Hurricanes Katrina and Rita, we ask that NEMA's members be consulted regarding further changes to the Department of Homeland Security and FEMA. Most importantly, consideration needs to be given to the connectivity between FEMA and the Preparedness Directorate within DHS, since all FEMA's preparedness functions were moved out into this new Directorate. When the Second Stage Review proposal was announced, NEMA articulated grave concern in a July 27, 2005 letter to the Department of Homeland Security regarding the Second Stage Review (2SR) creating a Preparedness Directorate that would be primarily focused on terrorism. The letter to Congress highlighted the lack of the Department's focus on natural-hazards preparedness and the inability to connect response and recovery operations to preparedness functions, as any unnecessary separation of these functions could result in a disjointed response and adversely impact the effectiveness of Departmental operations. Nevertheless, we understand that the 2SR is moving ahead and look forward to finding ways to connect the new Preparedness Directorate with FEMA. We fear that if those interrelationships are not made the result could mean that many state and local governments will be meeting FEMA for the first time when a disaster occurs in their state because of the separation of functions. We hope to work with Congress to ensure linkages of preparedness, response, recovery, and mitigation functions in the all-hazards approach to emergency management.

NEMA also calls on Congress to consider the needs of the FEMA in this year's budget process, to restore the agencies ability to respond to all disasters. Our nation is at the same point as it was after Hurricane Andrew in 1992, questioning organizational structures, leadership, the roles of federal, state, and local government, funding for FEMA and emergency management and even citizen preparedness. No federal agency is more qualified structurally and statutorily than FEMA to help our nation respond to and recover from disasters. FEMA has the direct relationships with state and local governments because of the grant programs and the disaster relief programs authorized through the Stafford Act. FEMA is the **only** federal agency authorized under the Robert T. Stafford Disaster Relief and Emergency Relief Act (42 U.S.C. 5121 et seq.) to carry out duties on behalf of the President. The 1978 Reorganization Plan 3, which created FEMA, also gives FEMA the responsibility for all of the functions of emergency preparedness and response. The plan states:

> "This reorganization rests on several fundamental principles. First, Federal authorities to anticipate, prepare for, and respond to major civil emergencies should be supervised by one official responsible to the President and given attention by other officials at the highest levels. The new agency would be in this position."

FEMA is and should be the agency of choice to coordinate the functions of the federal government in response to disasters, regardless of their cause.

FEMA has the ability to tap into the emergency responder community to build relationships through training and exercises. FEMA also has the skills to work cooperatively with state and local elected and appointed officials to work towards comprehensive recovery. FEMA has the coordinating function in the federal government and should have the ability to tap all the resources at the federal level to respond to a disaster. However, all these areas need to be strengthened with an all-hazards focus to ensure that federal, state, and local governments are building relationships before a disaster and understand how to work together cohesively. FEMA also needs financial support to maintain and build their capacity.

The time to stop the cycle of degradation of emergency management functions by reorganization after reorganization is now and we must systematically improve our nation's emergency response system through verified lessons learned and not reactionary decisions. We hope that Congress will partner with NEMA as they move forward to consider changes to DHS organizational functions and the role of FEMA.

CONCLUSION

The last year has proved our nation's continuous vulnerability against all-hazards of many sizes. We will be faced with recovery on the Gulf Coast for many years to come and we cannot ignore the predictions for the coming Hurricane season. We must continue to build national preparedness efforts with a multi-hazard approach. In this year's appropriations process Congress will make critical decisions that shape the future of emergency management in this country. As you begin your consideration, we ask you to recognize the importance of adequately funding the EMPG program in building capacity through people at the state and local level for all disasters. I thank you for the opportunity to testify on behalf of NEMA and appreciate your partnership.

Statement for the Record
Subcommittee on Homeland Security
Committee on Appropriations
United States House of Representatives
On the
Appropriations for the Department of Homeland Security for FY 2007

Michael D. Selves, CEM
First Vice President
International Association of Emergency Managers

March 16, 2006

Chairman Rogers, Ranking Member Sabo, and distinguished members of the Subcommittee, thank you for allowing me this opportunity to provide testimony on the President's FY 07 budget request for the Department of Homeland Security.

I am Michael D. Selves. I am currently the Emergency Management and Homeland Security Director for Johnson County, Kansas. Johnson County constitutes the Southwest suburbs of the Kansas City Metropolitan Area and, with a population of approximately a half million, is the most populous county in Kansas. I currently serve as the First Vice President of the International Association of Emergency Managers (IAEM) and am providing this testimony on their behalf. I am also a Certified Emergency Manager (CEM), and have served IAEM over the past five years as chair of the Government Affairs Committee. For the past 11 years I have been an active participant in the National Association of Counties, chairing their Subcommittee on Emergency Management, as a charter member of their Homeland Security Task Force as well as serving two years on their Board of Directors. I was appointed by Department of Homeland Security Secretary Ridge to his task force on state and local Homeland Security funding.

The International Association of Emergency Managers has over 2,700 members including emergency management professionals at the state and local government levels, the military, private business and the nonprofit sector in the United States and in other countries. Most of our members are city and county emergency managers who perform the crucial function of coordinating and integrating the efforts at the local level to prepare for, mitigate the effects of, respond to, and recover from all types of disasters including terrorist attacks. Our members include emergency managers from large urban areas as well as rural counties.

Hurricane Katrina has unequivocally demonstrated the need for strong emergency management programs at the federal state and local levels. As emergency management professionals, we know the only way plans, preparations and equipment can be brought to bear in a disaster is through the planning efforts - of people... people whose job it is to bring all elements of a community together to make the plans work and who will be there when the time comes to implement those plans. For this reason, we are limiting our statement to one single critical issue: We respectfully request your assistance in increasing the funding for the Emergency Management Program Grant (EMPG).

Emergency Management Performance Grant

- Request the $13,100,000 funding cut be rejected and the amount increased to $256 million to begin addressing the shortfall.
- Request that EMPG funding be maintained in a separate account as in the FY 06 Congressional action and not combined with other grant programs.

Increase funding for EMPG. Appropriations Committee report language referred to the program as "the backbone of the nation's emergency management system." In order to maintain this system and build the capacity required to meet the greatly increasing demands, additional investment is needed.

However, the President's Budget request for FY 2007 proposes to reduce the funding from the $183,100,000 appropriated in FY 06 to $170,000,000. According to a biennial study conducted by the National Emergency Management Association (NEMA) in 2004 there is a shortfall of $260 million. We respectfully request that EMPG be increased $86 million over the FY 07 request for a total of $256,000,000 to begin addressing this shortfall.

Maintain EMPG as a separate account. We also urge you to continue to maintain EMPG as a separate account. The President's budget includes this program in the "State and Local" account with a number of other grant programs. EMPG is different from the other programs in this account. EMPG has existed for over fifty years and supports all hazards emergency management, including terrorism. In addition, it is a performance based continuing program with deliverables and requirements that must be met in order to receive funding the next year.

EMPG is critically important. We believe it is the single most effective use of federal funds in providing emergency management capacity to state and local governments. No other source of homeland security funding is based on a consensus building process determining outcomes and specific deliverables backstopped by a quarterly accountability process. In fact, we feel this program would more accurately be described by the name Emergency Management Assistance

(EMA) because of the unique requirements for deliverables and accountability it imposes – unique among all other homeland security sources of financial assistance.

In addition, this unique program has never experienced "backlogs" of unspent funds because it is built on the experience and refinement of over five decades of proven effectiveness and efficiency. EMPG assistance requires a 50 percent state or local match, thus creating the much-needed "buy-in" not present in many other grant programs. Actually, the "buy-in" in this program is significantly greater due to the fact that currently many local jurisdictions are receiving 20% or less. In addition many local jurisdictions receive no funding at all because of shortage of funds.

Examples of the critical benefits of EMPG are the following:

- This program provides funding for the emergency managers who perform the role of the "honest broker" at the state and local level and who establish the emergency management framework for preparedness, response, recovery and mitigation.

- EMPG funding provides the people who are legally responsible for creating a "culture of preparedness" at the state and local level.

- EMPG funding also provides many of the personnel who can be deployed across state lines to assist other states in case of disaster through the Emergency Management Assistance Compact (EMAC). During the 2005 response to Hurricanes Katrina and Rita 65, 919 civilian and military personnel and equipment assets were deployed from 48 states, the District of Columbia, the Virgin Islands and Puerto Rico. Over 2100 missions were performed.

- EMPG funding has assumed a greater importance in light of recent catastrophic events and the responses to those events. For example, the President and the Department of Homeland Security (DHS) have tasked state and local government emergency managers with the responsibility to review their Emergency Operations Plans regarding the issue of evacuation.

- EMPG supports the people who have had the added responsibility of administering homeland security funding programs and additional planning efforts since 2001. While we agree the National Plan Review is a vitally important project, floods, tornadoes and other disasters simply haven't stopped happening.

Without more funding and people we can't reach the level of preparedness our nation deserves and our citizens demand.

The recent White House report on the response to the Hurricane Katrina contains 125 recommendations. A significant number of these recommendations are "top-down" initiatives which require the collaboration and coordination efforts of state and local emergency managers in order to be fully implemented. We also know that genuine solutions to broad based issues like emergency management can only succeed if they recognize the primary importance of state and local governments.

One way to sum things up is to acknowledge that beautiful plans written without the input and agreement of key stakeholders on roles and responsibilities will gather dust on shelves. A plan that works and has broad based buy in may be ugly and patched, but it lives, breathes and works, just like the people who implement it in a disaster.

EMPG provides people who build partnerships. The single most critically important thing EMPG funding provides is emergency management personnel at the state and local level. People are the most important investment this program makes because without them nothing else works. Emergency Management is a people process. I would like to point to my own jurisdiction – Johnson County, Kansas – as an example.

Even before Katrina, we were engaged in the process of evaluating and revising our local emergency operations plan. I can tell you that this plan truly has broad buy in and acceptance within our jurisdiction. This happened because 16 subcommittees involving more than 120 people for 8 months of effort developed the 16 annexes of our plan. Because of the extensively and intensively people-based approach of this process, all of our officials – from our elected local leadership and senior management to front-line first responders – know and accept their roles and responsibilities. This would not have happened without EMPG funding providing the personnel in my office to facilitate this process. And the end result is very important. **If we shake hands before the disaster, we won't have to point fingers afterwards.**

Emergency Management personnel at the state and local level have long involved private enterprise and faith-based groups in their inclusive, all-hazards planning process. For example, many of the state and local governments that hosted Katrina survivors fully integrated private and faith based organizations in their reception planning. These organizations' contributions ranged from providing critically needed supplies to serving as counselors and community emissaries for potential new residents of our communities.

In conclusion, we believe this program must be maintained and sustained at a level which ensures that we continue to have a strong, truly national, system of emergency management in America. I sincerely thank you for this opportunity to express our deep concerns.

Contact

IAEM Headquarters ▪ 201 Park Washington Court, Falls Church, VA 22043 www.iaem.com
Martha Braddock, IAEM Policy Advisory, 703-644-7082, braddock@iaem.com
Michael D. Selves, CEM, IAEM First Vice President, 913-782-3038, mselves@jocogov.org

ASCE

American Society of Civil Engineers

Washington Office
101 Constitution Ave., N.W.
Suite 375 East
Washington, D.C. 20001
(202) 789-7850
Fax: (202) 789-7859
Web: http://www.asce.org

**Testimony of the
AMERICAN SOCIETY OF CIVIL ENGINEERS
on the Proposed Budget for Fiscal Year 2007
for the Department of Homeland Security
before the
Subcommittee on Homeland Security
Committee on Appropriations
U. S. House of Representatives
March 16, 2006**

The American Society of Civil Engineers (ASCE) is pleased to offer testimony on the President's proposed FY 2007 budget for the Department of Homeland Security. ASCE would like to specifically address the Dam Safety Program, the National Earthquake Hazards Reduction Program and the National Windstorm Impact Reduction Program.

ASCE, founded in 1852, is the country's oldest national civil engineering organization representing 139,000 civil engineers in private practice, government, industry and academia dedicated to the advancement of the science and profession of civil engineering. ASCE is a 501(c) (3) non-profit educational and professional society.

I. The National Dam Safety Program

ASCE respectfully requests that the Subcommittee increase the Administration's proposed budget of $5.9 million to $8.6 million to fully fund the National Dam Safety Program at its authorized level for FY 2007. ASCE further requests that there be a line item in the DHS budget that clearly identifies the funds be used to carry out mandates authorized in the National Dam Safety and Security Act of 2002.

The National Dam Safety Program Act of 1996 (PL 104-303) created the first national program that focused on improving the safety of the nation's dams. Congress reauthorized the program through the Dam Safety and Security Act of 2002 (PL 107-310) and made modest increases in the authorized funds. This small yet critical program provides much needed assistance to the state dam safety programs in the form of grant assistance, training and research; and through facilitating the exchange of technical information between federal dam safety partners and the states. The program provides $6 million in grant assistance to states based on the relative number of dams in each state. The grants may be utilized to best suit the individual state's needs. In addition, the National Dam Safety Program provides $500,000 each year to be used for training of state dam safety engineers and $1.5 million annually for research. These research funds are used to identify more effective methods of evaluating the safety of dams and more efficient techniques to repair dams. And now, these research funds can be used to develop better methods to assess and improve the security of dams.

There are over 79,000 dams in the United States, but the responsibility of assuring their safety falls largely on the shoulders of the states, as they regulate 95% of the country's dams. Because of limited staff and funding, most states are overwhelmed by that challenge. Currently states have identified over 3,300 dams as being deficient, or unsafe. The number of unsafe dams has risen by 33% since 1998. Unsafe means that they have identified deficiencies that make the dam more susceptible to failure, which may be triggered by a large storm event, an earthquake or simply through inadequate maintenance or outdated protection standards.

There are over 10,000 dams classified as high hazard potential meaning that the consequences of the dam's failure will likely include loss of human life and significant downstream property damage. According to the National Inventory of Dams, more than 53% of the high hazard potential dams have not been inspected in the last ten years. High hazard potential dams should be inspected every year.

ASCE's 2005 Report Card for America's Infrastructure gave Dams in the United States a grade of "D." The dams across the United States are aging as 85% of the dams will be 50 years or older by the year 2020.

Downstream development within the dam failure flood zone places more people at risk. When homes are built in the dam failure flood zone below a low hazard dam, (low hazard: failure is not expected to cause loss of life or significant property damage) the dam no longer meets dam safety criteria as the potential consequences of a failure now include loss of life.

There is a clear need for continued federal leadership to provide assistance in support of dam safety. This country suffered several large and tragic dam failures in the 1970s that focused attention on dams and prompted Congress to pass national dam safety legislation. In 1972, the Buffalo Creek Dam in West Virginia failed and killed 125 individuals; in 1976 the Teton Dam failure in Idaho caused $1 billion in damages and 14 deaths; the Kelly Barnes Dam in Toccao Falls, Georgia failed in 1977 killing 39 Bible college students; also in 1977 40 people died from the failure of the Laurel Run Dam in Pennsylvania; and in 1996 the 38 foot tall Meadow Pond Dam in Alton, New Hampshire failed killing one woman and causing $8 million in damage.

The National Dam Safety Program has been very successful in assisting the state programs. The training program is one aspect of this success ($500,000). This training provides access to technical courses and workshops that state engineers could not otherwise attend. Examples include Dambreak Analysis, Concrete Rehabilitation of Dams, Slope Stability of Dams, Earthquake Analysis, Emergency Action Planning and many others including recent training in Dam Site Security. Training courses are also offered through FEMA's training facility at their Emergency Management Institute in Maryland where state dam safety inspectors receive training at no cost to the states.

The Research Program is an important program to all within the dam safety community. Its funds have been used to identify future research needs such as inspections using ground penetrating radar or risk analysis. In addition, these funds have been used to create a national library and database of dam failures and dam statistics at the National Performance of Dams Program at

Stanford University as well as a national clearinghouse and library of dam safety bibliographic data at ASDSO.

Research funds are currently being used to provide security training, security assessment tools and best management practices for states to utilize in addressing potential terrorists actions against the 75,000 non-federal dams. The small increase ($500,000) in the funding levels authorized by the 2002 act was intended to address dam site security. Dam site security is now an urgent area of concern for state dam safety officials both in training needs and in research to better understand and respond to potential threats to dams.

It is disappointing to see that appropriations over the past two years are well below the authorized levels, just as we begin to realize the benefits of the grant assistance program—dam safety inspections have increased, the number of Emergency Action Plans, used to notify and evacuate downstream populations in the event of a failure, have increased. Despite the increase in funding approved by Congress in the Dam Safety and Security Act of 2002 to $8.6 million, appropriations have remained at the previous level of $5.9 million. States have not realized any increase in assistance. Budget reductions at FEMA have further reduced the state grant assistance funds by almost 22%.

II. The National Earthquake Hazards Reduction Program (NEHRP)

For the past 30 years NEHRP has provided the resources and leadership that have led to significant advances in understanding the risks earthquakes pose and the best ways to counter them. ASCE is pleased with the Administration's requested increase of $29.4 million to $233.5 million for readiness, mitigation and recovery and the requested increase of $99 million to $149.9 for the National Pre-disaster Mitigation program within FEMA.

ASCE supports the President's requests and supports the inclusion of a line item in the appropriations to the full funding level contained in the reauthorization for FY 2007 of $22.3 million for NEHRP responsibilities at the Federal Emergency Management Agency (FEMA). This would include $2.2 million for the creation of performance based earthquake standards.

Under NEHRP, there has been a constant source of funding for seismic monitoring, mapping, research, testing, code development, mitigation and emergency preparedness. It has served as the backbone for protecting U.S. citizens, their property and the national economy from the devastating effects of large earthquakes. Although NEHRP is well known for its research programs, it is also the source for hundreds of new technologies, maps, design techniques and standards that are used by design professionals every day to mitigate hazards risks that will save lives, protect property, and reduce adverse economic impacts.

NEHRP is of direct benefit to homeland security. It provides a framework for safeguarding our communities from a multitude of threats that include natural hazards, severe accidents, and terrorism. It is the source for hundreds of new technologies, maps, design techniques, and construction standards. In spite of all the good activities that have been stimulated and supported by NEHRP, the United States continues to face an earthquake risk that is unacceptably high and growing. FEMA estimates that 45 states and territories are destined to experience earthquake damage. This exposure has been estimated to equal an annualized loss of over $6 billion per year, with a single event loss potential of $100 to $200 billion and tens of thousands of casualties. (FEMA 2001, adjusted to 2004 dollars) NEHRP's ability to expand monitoring, research and the development of tools that will significantly improve the nation's ability to address the problem is limited by the funds that have been appropriated and actually spent on earthquake mitigation.

The earthquakes that have affected the United States during the past 20 years have demonstrated that the nation needs to reconsider how much damage is acceptable in a major earthquake. Traditional thinking has held that communities need only assure that people are safe and able to exit damaged buildings after the shaking stops, with little regard to the economic disruption caused by the destruction. Current thinking recognizes that higher performance objectives are appropriate for certain classes of buildings. For example, hospitals and emergency response support facilities, transportation systems and other infrastructure networks should be designed to remain operational. High value manufacturing facilities should be designed to be easily repairable and residential construction should be designed to remain safe to occupy. These changes have led to the emergence of Performance Based Earthquake Engineering design standards that direct development of cost effective and affordable solutions in the design of buildings to predictable performance levels. Nearly $1 trillion dollars is spent each year on the construction of buildings, transportation, and infrastructure systems in the United States. The total value of construction in the nation is about $7.5 trillion dollars. The development of new performance based engineering standards will directly affect the safety and reliability of this extraordinary investment in new and existing construction.

The American Society of Civil Engineers, along with other members of the NEHRP Coalition, worked closely with members and staff in both the House and Senate in crafting the five year reauthorization of NEHRP through H.R. 2608, which became P.L. 108-360. We strongly support the results and believe that, when fully carried out, the changes made and funding levels set under the new law will support and stimulate significant new mitigation activities that will result in reduced vulnerability to earthquake hazards and a real and significant reduction in the loss of life and property. It will also result in the savings of hundreds of millions of dollars in Federal disaster relief spending.

III. The Windstorm Impact Reduction Program

In October 2004 the President signed Public Law 108-360 which authorized the creation of a National Windstorm Impact Reduction Program. As the representatives of the profession most responsible for mitigating the impact of high wind, we know full well the benefits this program holds for the nation. As last year's events on the nation's gulf coast have so vividly illustrated, the nation remains highly vulnerable to major windstorms. We have not yet fully calculated the full damage inflicted by Hurricanes Katrina, Rita and Wilma, but it could well exceed $150 billion.

For Fiscal Year 2007 the law authorizes $25 million in spending, spread between four federal four agencies. ASCE urges Congress to support these funding levels. Specifically, for the agency under the jurisdiction of this subcommittee, the law authorizes $9.4 million for the Federal Emergency Management Agency (FEMA).

This legislation represents five years of work in which stake holders representing a broad cross-section of interests such as the research, technology transfer, design and construction, and financial communities; materials and systems suppliers; state, county, and local governments; and the insurance industry have participated in crafting this legislation. This bill represents a consensus of all those with an interest in the issue and a desire to see the benefits this legislation will generate. ASCE worked closely with members and staff in both the House and Senate in crafting the language contained in H.R. 2608, which became P.L. 108-360. We strongly support the results and believe that, if fully carried out, the new law will result in reduced vulnerability to high winds and will lead to real and significant reduction in the loss of life and property. The United States currently sustains billions of dollars per year in property and economic loss due to windstorms. The Federal government's response to such events is to initiate search and rescue operations, help clear the debris and provide financial assistance for rebuilding. With this legislation, the Federal government can provide increased research funding to mobilize the technical expertise already available and help reduce the significant annual toll in casualties and property damage from windstorms.

Under the authorization, the FEMA is charged with supporting the development of risk assessment tools and effective mitigation techniques, windstorm-related data collection and analysis, public outreach, information dissemination, and implementation of mitigation measures consistent with the Agency's all-hazards approach.

Association of State Dam Safety Officials
450 Old Vine Street, 2nd Floor
Lexington, Kentucky 40507
Phone: (859) 257-5140
Fax: (859) 323-1958
www.damsafety.org

Testimony of the
ASSOCIATION OF STATE DAM SAFETY OFFICIALS
on the Proposed Budget for Fiscal Year 2007
for the Department of Homeland Security
before the
Subcommittee on Homeland Security
Committee on Appropriations
U.S. House of Representatives
March 16, 2006

Dear Chairman Rogers and Members of the Subcommittee:

The Association of State Dam Safety Officials (ASDSO) is pleased to offer testimony on the President's proposed FY 2007 budget for the Department of Homeland Security.

The Association of State Dam Safety Officials respectfully requests that the Subcommittee increase the Administration's proposed budget of $5.9 million to $8.6 million to fully fund the National Dam Safety Program at its authorized level for FY 2007. The Association further requests that these funds be earmarked for the sole purpose of carrying out mandates authorized in the National Dam Safety and Security Act of 2002.

The Association of State Dam Safety Officials is a national organization of more than 2,200 state, federal and local dam safety professionals and private sector individuals dedicated to improving dam safety through research, education and technology transfer. ASDSO represents the 50 state dam safety programs, as the state dam safety officials are the governing body of the Association. Our goal is simply to save lives, prevent property damage and to maintain the many benefits of dams by preventing dam failures.

During the 1970s this country suffered devastating dam failures that caused tragic loss of life and enormous property damage; and focused national attention on the catastrophic consequences of dam failures. Those historic failures and recent dam failures serve as a constant reminder that dams must always be properly constructed, properly designed and properly operated and maintained to provide vital benefits and prevent failures.

Today our focus in not only on the safety of dams related to maintenance issues but on security as the nation faces a significant challenge to protect our infrastructure from terrorist attacks. Protection of U.S. dams is a major concern and focus of national strategic planning efforts within the Department of Homeland Security.

National Dam Safety Program

The National Dam Safety Program Act of 1996 (PL 104-303) created the first national program that focused on improving the safety of the nation's dams. Congress reauthorized the program through the Dam Safety and Security Act of 2002 (PL 107-310) and made modest increases in the authorized funds. This small, yet critical program provides much needed assistance to the state dam safety programs in the form of grant assistance, training and research; and through facilitating the exchange of technical information between federal dam safety partners and the states. As authorized, the program provides $6 million in grant assistance to states based on the relative number of dams in each state. The grants may be utilized to best suit the individual state's needs. In addition, the National Dam Safety Program provides $500,000 each year to be used for training of state dam safety engineers and $1.5 million annually for research. These research funds are used to identify more effective methods of evaluating the safety of dams and more efficient techniques to repair dams. And now, these research funds can be used to develop better methods to assess and improve the security of dams.

There are over 79,000 dams in the United States, but the responsibility of assuring their safety falls on the shoulders of the states, as they regulate 95% of the country's dams. Because of limited staff and limited funding, most states are overwhelmed by that challenge. Table 1 attached to this testimony provides state-by-state data on the number of dams, the number of staff, the state budget and the number of dams that are considered "unsafe." Unsafe means that they have identified deficiencies that make the dam more susceptible to failure, which may be triggered by a large storm event, an earthquake or simply through inadequate maintenance or outdated protection standards. Currently states have identified over 3,500 dams as being deficient, or unsafe. The number of unsafe dams has risen by 33% since 1998. In Kentucky the state lists 88 unsafe dams including 36 that are classified as high hazard potential. In Pennsylvania there are 531 unsafe dams and 98 of these are classified as high hazard potential.

There are over 10,000 dams classified as high hazard potential meaning that the consequences of the dam's failure will likely include loss of human life and significant downstream property damage. Every member of this Subcommittee has high hazard dams in their home state. There are 175 high hazard potential dams in Kentucky, 861 high hazard potential dams in Texas and 1046 high hazard potential dams in North Carolina. According to the National Inventory of Dams more than 53% of the high hazard potential dams have not been inspected in the last ten years. High hazard potential dams should be inspected every year.

The task for state dam safety programs is staggering; in Iowa where there are over 3,300 dams there are only 1.25 full time employees assigned to the dam safety program. Texas has over 8,100 dams with only 5 engineers in their dam safety program; and Minnesota, which has more than 1,400 dams, only has a staff of 2.1 full time employees

The America Society of Civil Engineer's 2005 Report Card for America's Infrastructure gave Dams in the United States a grade of "D." The dams across the United States are aging as 85% of the dams will be 50 years or older by the year 2020.

Downstream development within the dam failure flood zone places more people at risk. When homes are built in the dam failure flood zone below a low hazard dam, (low hazard: failure is not expected to cause loss of life or significant property damage) the dam no longer meets dam safety criteria as the potential consequences of a failure now include loss of life.

Federal Leadership Role

There is a clear need for continued federal leadership to provide assistance in support of dam safety. This country suffered several large and tragic dam failures in the 1970s that focused attention on dams and prompted Congress to pass national dam safety legislation. In 1972, the Buffalo Creek Dam in West Virginia failed and killed 125 individuals; in 1976 the Teton Dam failure in Idaho caused $1 billion in damages and 14 deaths; the Kelly Barnes Dam in Toccao Falls, Georgia failed in 1977 killing 39 Bible college students; also in 1977 40 people died from the failure of the Laurel Run Dam in Pennsylvania; and in 1996 the 38 foot tall Meadow Pond Dam in Alton, New Hampshire failed killing one woman and causing $8 million in damage.

However, the failure of the Silver Lake Dam in Michigan in May 2003 again demonstrated the enormous potential damages that dam failures can produce. This dam failure caused more than $100 million in damages including $10 million in damages to utilities, $4 million to the environment, $3 million to roads and bridges and flooded 20 homes and businesses. In addition, the Silver Lake Dam failure flooded a major power plant, which in turn caused the closure of two iron mines, putting 1,100 miners temporarily out of work.

In March 2006, the Kaloko Reservoir dam burst in Hawaii on the island of Kaua'I releasing more than 300 million gallons of water killing seven people and washing was a number of farm buildings and houses.

In March 2004, the Big Bay Lake Dam in Mississippi failed destroying 48 homes, damaging 53 homes, 2 churches, three businesses and a fire station and washing out a bridge. This dam, which cost $2.5 million to construct, has caused many millions in damages, will require downstream homeowners and businesses to rebuild, caused significant loss of property values around the lake and has resulted in $100 million lawsuit filed against the dam owner on behalf of the homeowners.

In the past two years, 29 dam failures were reported to the National Performance of Dams program, which collects and archives information on dam performance as reported by state and federal regulatory agencies and dam owners.

Dam failures do not respect state boundaries, as a dam failure in one state may cause loss of life and property damage in an adjacent state. Including recovery costs from the President's disaster relief fund and the Flood Insurance Program, the cost of one small dam failure can easily exceed the annual costs of the National Dam Safety Program. Full funding of the National Dam Safety Program is an investment in public safety that will be repaid many times over in fewer dam failures, reduced federal expenditures for dam failure recovery and, most importantly, fewer lives lost.

Benefits of the National Dam Safety Program

The National Dam Safety Program has been very successful in assisting the state programs. The training program is one aspect of this success ($500,000). This training provides access to technical courses and workshops that state engineers could not otherwise attend. Examples include Dambreak Analysis, Concrete Rehabilitation of Dams, Slope Stability of Dams, Earthquake Analysis, Emergency Action Planning and many others including recent training in Dam Site Security. Training courses are also offered through FEMA's training facility at their Emergency Management Institute in Maryland where state dam safety inspectors receive training at no cost to the states.

The Research Program is an important program to all within the dam safety community. Its funds have been used to identify future research needs such as inspections using ground penetrating radar or risk analysis. In addition, these funds have been used to create a national library and database of dam failures and dam statistics at the National Performance of Dams Program at Stanford University as well as a national clearinghouse and library of dam safety bibliographic data at ASDSO.

Research funds are currently being used to provide security training, security assessment tools and best management practices for states to utilize in addressing potential terrorists actions against the 75,000 non-federal dams. The small increase ($500,000) in the funding levels authorized by the 2002 act was intended to address dam site security. Dam site security is now an urgent area of concern for state dam safety officials both in training needs and in research to better understand and respond to potential threats to dams.

The most valuable benefit to the state programs comes from the State Grant Assistance Program. The grants are based on the number of dams in each of the participating states and are used as an incentive to encourage states to improve their program by meeting basic criteria such as:

- State statutory authority to conduct inspections of dams;
- State authority to require repairs to unsafe dams; or
- State policies that address dam site security at non-federal dams.

Use of these grants is left up to the state's discretion as each state has its own unique challenges. States have utilized grant funds to perform dam failure and dam stability analyses, to hire additional staff to conduct inspections and to conduct owner education workshops. In addition, grant funds have enabled states to provide additional staff training, and to purchase equipment such as computers, field survey equipment and software, and remote operated cameras for internal inspections.

It is disappointing to see that appropriations over the past two years are well below the authorized levels, just as we begin to realize the benefits of the grant assistance program—dam safety inspections have increased, the number of Emergency Action Plans, used to notify and evacuate downstream populations in the event of a failure, have increased. Despite the increase in funding approved by Congress in the Dam Safety and Security Act of 2002 to $8.6 million, appropriations have remained at the previous level of $5.9 million. States have not realized any increase in assistance. Budget reductions at FEMA have further reduced the state grant assistance funds by almost 22%.

Table 2, attached to this testimony, provides information on the amount of state grant assistance received for each state, the potential grant funding if fully funded at authorized levels and the grant amount each state will lose as a result of the reduced funding. The lost grants come at a difficult time when development below dams creates additional high hazard potential dams, dams continue to age and, now, security issues must be addressed by the states.

Dam Security of Non-Federal Dams

The events of September 11, 2001 have focused unprecedented attention on the security of our nation's critical infrastructure, including dams. Dams, in fact, have been identified by intelligence and law enforcement agencies in specific threat alerts. Federal agencies that own dams, such as the US Army Corps of Engineers and the Bureau of Reclamation, have been conducting vulnerability assessments and security improvements on these federally owned dams. However, federal government expertise or assistance to the states, which have similar and equally urgent dam security demands, has not been forthcoming.

The improved security at federally owned dams makes non-federal dams more attractive targets. There are clearly thousands of non-federal dams that are potential targets based on type of construction, size, purpose (water supply, hydro power, flood control); and on the population and infrastructure at risk below the dam. Federal leadership is urgently needed to provide technical and financial assistance to states for training, for conducting vulnerability assessments and for identifying and implementing security improvements on dams determined to have an inadequate security program.

Conclusion

Dams are a vital part of our aging national infrastructure that provide many vital benefits, but that also pose a threat to life and property if they fail. The National Dam Safety Program is a valuable program that offers assistance to states as an investment in public safety. One dam failure alone, as evidenced by the Silver Lake Dam failure in 2003, can easily exceed the $8.6 million authorized for this program. The National Dam Safety Program, administered by FEMA, is a modest and prudent investment protecting public safety.

Therefore, ASDSO respectfully requests that this Subcommittee increase the Administration's proposed funding for the National Dam Safety Program from $5.9 million to the full authorized level of $8.6 million; and further earmark these funds to be used only for the National Dam Safety Program in the Department of Homeland Security.

ASDSO looks forward to working with the Subcommittee staff to improve the safety of dams.

Association of State Dam Safety Officials
State-By-State Statistics on Dams and State Safety Regulation – Dec 2004

State	Total Dams in National Inventory[1]	Dams Under State Regulation[2]		State-Determined Deficient Dams[3]			State Dam Safety Budget	State Staff Dedicated to Dam Safety Regulation	
	(2002 NID)	Total	HH	Total	HH	SH	(x thousand)	Total FTEs	Dams Per FTE
Alabama	2,102	0	171	NA	-	-	$0	0	NA
Alaska	104	81	18	29	7	7	$86.8	1.0	81
Arizona	328	259	91	38	33	5	$606.7	7.5	35
Arkansas	1,225	407	102	24	22	1	$331.0	4.6	88
California	1,471	1,259	336	44*	24	16	$7,800.0	61.0	21
Colorado	1,684	1,897	332	186	24	36	$1,400.0	12.0	158
Connecticut	721	2,200	238	22	9	10	$472	4.3	512
Delaware	61	98	9	NR	-	-	NR	NR	NR
Florida	724	778*	100*	>20	NR	NR	NR	NR	NR
Georgia	4,470	3,412	399	105	NR	NR	$682.0	8.0	341
Hawaii	122	134	77	22	20	2	$140.0	1.75	77
Idaho	393	429	95	13	3	6	$300.0	7.5	57
Illinois	1,456	1,348	176	31	21	10	$345.0	5.5	245
Indiana	1,069	1,089	238	NR	-	-	$340.0	5.0	218
Iowa	3,249	3,303	74	25	9	12	$50.0	1.75	1,887
Kansas	5,634	5,877	192	42	17	15	$327.3	7.0	840
Kentucky	1,055	918	175	88	36	35	$1,600.0	14.0	66
Louisiana	501	500	17	16	1	3	NR	7.0	71
Maine	641	843	26*	68	7	33	$46.0*	1.1	766
Maryland	291	369	64	12	5	2	$445.7	5.5	67
Massachusetts	1,490	2,917	333	40	22	18	$500.0	4.0	729
Michigan	943	988	79	25	5	9	$454.0	4.8	206
Minnesota	986	1,442	40	250	2	20	$250.0	2.1	687
Mississippi	3,315	3,592	307	36	36	-	$375.0	3.85	933
Missouri	4,854	643	447	16	13	2	$281.8	6.0	107
Montana	2,885	2,878	102	>11	11	NR	$412.0	5.25	548
Nebraska	2,179	2,173	113	130	7	48	$289.0	5.67	383
Nevada	469	610	134	>58	4	4	NR	2.25	271
New Hamp.	645	3,348	86	357	31	90	$563.6	7.5	446
New Jersey	792	1,692	196	583	47	336	$1,251.0	19.0	89
New Mexico	375	393	164	61	38	14	$409.0	6.0	66
New York	1964	5,021	383	>54	NR	NR	$746.0	5.3	947
North Carolina	2723	4,661	1,046	>81	55	>14	$910.0	17	274
North Dakota	685	1,182**	20	17	5	10	$200.0	4.5	263
Ohio	1,325	1,727	462	NR	-	-	$1,020.0	11.0	157
Oklahoma	4,610	4,506	185	31	8	3	$122.4	2.5	1802
Oregon	820	3,733	122	0	0	0	$255.0	3.1	1,204
Pennsylvania	1,442	3,089	768	~725	266	43	$2,039.0	24.0	129
Puerto Rico	34	35	34	0	0	0	$650.0	9.0	4
Rhode Island	185	565	17	0	0	0	$104.9	1.2	471
South Carolina	2,447	2,313	153	>3	1	2	NR	2.5	925
South Dakota	2,377	2,328	47	3	3	NR	NR	2.5	931
Tennessee	1,051	637	147	8	2	2	$275.0	7.0	91
Texas	7,025	7,490	857	113	108	3	$300.0	6.0	1,248
Utah	752	667	192	82	82	NR	$460.0	7.0	93
Vermont	353	565	57	NR	-	-	$235.0	2.4	235
Virginia	1,586	1,363	126	74	34	25	$546.3	4.5	303
Washington	832	940	140	31	14	17	$660.0	7.5	125
West Virginia	553	477	366	38	35	3	$469.9	6.0	79.5
Wisconsin	1,097	3,748	187	NR	-	-	$508.7	6.25	600
Wyoming	1,294	1,392	79	3	0	1	$142.1	5.09	273.5
TOTAL (12/04)	79,389	92,316	10,319	>3,615	1067	857	$29,402.2	355.26	260 (av)
TOTAL (3/04)	79,272	92,231	10,159	>3,341	667	855	$28,864.8	3589.24	257 (av.)

1 – Includes dams of any size that are likely to pose a significant threat to human life or property in case of failure, and all other federal and non-federal dams > 25' high that impound > 15 acre-feet; and dams > 6' high that impound > 50 acre-feet.
2 – Estimated number of all dams under state regulatory control
3 - Dams with identified deficiencies by state definition (varies state to state) derived from state inventory in column 2
*CA: California defines a deficiency as a dam requiring action to be taken to repair/resolve a safety problem (not including maintenance items). However in no case is the dam susceptible to failure. In the most severe cases a restriction is in place so a failure will not occur.
**State no longer regulates low hazard dams impounding less than 50 acre-ft.

Table 2 FEMA National Dam Safety Program State Grant Assistance Funds
Reduced Grant amounts in FY 2003 and FY 2004, Grants at full funding and
Estimated cumulative state grant losses over four year period FY 2003 through FY 2006

STATE	FY 2003 Reduced Grant Authorized at $ 6 M Appropriated at $4 M	FY 2004 Reduced Grant Authorized at $ 6 M Appropriated at $4 M	FY 2003-2006 Annual Grant if fully funded at $ 6 M	FY 2003 & 2004 Lost grant assistance over past two years	FY 2003 thru FY 2006 Projected grant loss over four years at current levels
Alabama*	$0	$0	$0	$0	$0
Alaska	$25,715	$22,990	$44,091	-$39,477	-$81,680
Arizona	$29,834	$26,672	$51,153	-$45,800	-$94,762
Arkansas	$35,898	$32,093	$61,550	-$55,109	-$114,022
California	$64,139	$57,340	$109,971	-$98,463	-$203,724
Colorado	$74,716	$66,797	$128,108	-$114,702	-$237,323
Connecticut	$46,113	$41,226	$79,065	-$70,791	-$146,470
Delaware*	$0	$0	$0	$0	$0
Florida	$41,730	$37,307	$71,550	-$64,063	-$132,548
Georgia	$144,571	$129,248	$247,880	-$221,940	-$459,204
Hawaii	$27,099	$24,227	$46,464	-$41,602	-$86,076
Idaho	$36,886	$32,977	$63,245	-$56,626	-$117,162
Illinois	$64,303	$57,487	$110,253	-$98,716	-$204,247
Indiana	$61,074	$54,601	$104,717	-$93,758	-$193,990
Iowa	$123,487	$110,398	$211,728	-$189,572	-$392,232
Kansas	$229,727	$205,378	$393,887	-$352,668	-$729,686
Kentucky	$56,460	$50,476	$96,806	-$86,675	-$179,335
Louisiana	$33,064	$29,559	$56,691	-$50,759	-$105,022
Maine	$43,774	$39,134	$75,054	-$67,200	-$139,040
Maryland	$35,371	$31,622	$60,647	-$54,300	-$112,349
Massachuettes	$74,485	$66,590	$127,712	-$114,347	-$236,589
Michigan	$44,993	$40,224	$77,144	-$69,071	-$142,910
Minnesota	$50,726	$45,350	$86,975	-$77,873	-$161,123
Mississippi	$135,482	$121,121	$232,295	-$207,986	-$430,332
Missouri	$43,280	$38,692	$74,207	-$66,441	-$137,470
Montana	$117,226	$104,801	$200,994	-$179,961	-$372,347
Nebraska	$90,205	$80,644	$154,664	-$138,479	-$286,518
Nevada	$36,063	$32,241	$61,833	-$55,362	-$114,547
New Hampshire	$49,639	$44,377	$85,110	-$76,204	-$157,669
New Jersey	$76,002	$67,946	$130,311	-$116,675	-$241,405
New Mexico	$37,842	$33,831	$64,884	-$58,094	-$120,199
New York	$87,074	$77,844	$149,295	-$133,672	-$276,573
North Carolina	$164,711	$147,253	$282,411	-$252,858	-$523,174
North Dakota	$41,368	$36,983	$70,929	-$63,507	-$131,398
Ohio	$79,857	$71,393	$136,922	-$122,593	-$253,651
Oklahoma	$170,676	$152,585	$292,638	-$262,015	-$542,120
Oregon	$61,634	$55,101	$105,677	-$94,618	-$195,769
Pennsylvania	$63,678	$56,928	$109,181	-$97,755	-$202,260
Puerto Rico	$24,031	$21,484	$41,204	-$36,892	-$76,331
Rhode Island	$31,097	$27,801	$53,319	-$47,739	-$98,775
South Carolina	$96,762	$86,506	$165,906	-$148,545	-$307,345
South Dakota	$97,619	$87,272	$167,376	-$149,861	-$310,069
Tennessee	$42,027	$37,572	$72,059	-$64,518	-$133,490
Texas	$245,643	$219,607	$421,176	-$377,102	-$780,240
Utah	$40,314	$36,041	$69,122	-$61,888	-$128,049
Vermont	$33,986	$30,384	$58,272	-$52,174	-$107,950
Virginia	$38,930	$34,804	$66,749	-$59,764	-$123,653
Washington	$40,215	$35,952	$68,952	-$61,736	-$127,735
West Virginia	$33,064	$29,559	$56,691	-$50,759	-$105,022
Wisconsin	$54,681	$48,885	$93,755	-$83,943	-$173,683
Wyoming	$67,632	$60,463	$115,961	-$103,826	-$214,820

* No state dam safety program

NEHRP Coalition

National Earthquake Hazards Reduction Program Coalition

American Council of Engineering Companies ♦ American Geological Institute ♦ American Geophysical Union ♦ American Institute of Architects ♦ American Public Works Association ♦ American Society of Civil Engineers ♦ Consortium of Universities for Research in Earthquake Engineering ♦ Earthquake Engineering Research Institute ♦ International Code Council ♦ Manufactured Housing Association for Regulatory Reform ♦ National Fire Protection Association ♦ Portland Cement Association ♦ Seismological Society of America

For More Information:
202/789-7850 (ASCE)
510/451-0905 (EERI)
www.nehrp.org

♦♦♦♦♦♦♦

The NEHRP Coalition encourages realistic, comprehensive, and affordable measures to reduce the harmful effects of earthquakes nationwide. The Coalition represents the views of over 250,000 scientists, engineers, architects, and emergency response leaders of the earthquake community.

Statement Of National Earthquake Hazards Reduction Program (NEHRP) Coalition Before the Subcommittee on Homeland Security Committee on Appropriations U.S. House of Representatives On the Budget for Federal Emergency Management Agency For the Fiscal Year 2007

In October 2004, the President signed Public Law 108-360, reauthorizing the National Earthquake Hazards Reduction Program (NEHRP) for five years. As the representatives of the professions most responsible for mitigating the affects of earthquakes, we know the benefits this program holds for the nation. An integral part of NEHRP is the Federal Emergency Management Agency (FEMA) at the Department of Homeland Security.

The NEHRP Coalition would like to acknowledge and support increases for FEMA in the President's FY 2007 budget request for Readiness, Mitigation, Response and Recovery of $233 million, an increase of $29 million over FY 2006 and the $99 million increase in the National Predisaster Mitigation Program to $149 million.

The NEHRP Coalition supports the inclusion of a line item in the appropriations to the full funding level contained in the reauthorization for FY 2007 of $22.3 million for NEHRP responsibilities at the Federal Emergency Management Agency (FEMA). This would include $2.2 million for the creation of performance based earthquake standards.

The NEHRP Coalition

The Coalition represents the views of over 250,000 earthquake professionals - scientists, engineers, architects, and emergency response leaders of the earthquake community. The NEHRP Coalition encourages the continuing development of comprehensive, realistic, and affordable measures for reducing the harmful effects of earthquakes to acceptable levels nationwide.

The National Earthquake Hazards Reduction Program

For the past 30 years NEHRP has provided the resources and leadership that have led to significant advances in understanding the risk earthquakes pose and the best ways to counter them. As passed by Congress and signed by the President, the reauthorization will not only allow this important work to continue, but represents an opportunity to make greater improvements in the nation's efforts to mitigate the effects of earthquakes.

Under NEHRP, there has been a constant source of funding for seismic monitoring, mapping, research, testing, engineering and related reference materials for code development, mitigation and emergency preparedness. It has served as the backbone for protecting U.S. citizens, their property and the national economy from the devastating effects of large earthquakes. Although NEHRP is well known for its research programs, it is also the source for hundreds of new technologies, maps, design techniques and standards that are used by design professionals every day to mitigate hazards risks that will save lives, protect property, and reduce adverse economic impacts.

NEHRP is of direct benefit to homeland security. It provides a framework for safeguarding our communities from a multitude of threats that include natural hazards, severe accidents, and terrorism. It is the source for hundreds of new technologies, maps, design techniques, and construction standards. Under NEHRP, FEMA has been able to leverage a small amount of funding into an impressive series of design procedures, best practices, protective devices and codes.

Performance based engineering standards can lead to the mitigation of the damage from earthquakes to acceptable levels, and need to remain a focus of the reauthorization of NEHRP. The earthquakes that have affected the United States during the past 20 years have demonstrated that the nation needs to reconsider how much damage is acceptable in a major earthquake. Traditional thinking has held that communities need only assure that people are safe and able to exit damaged buildings after the shaking stops, with little regard to the economic disruption caused by the destruction. Current thinking recognizes that higher performance objectives are appropriate for certain classes of buildings. For example, hospitals and emergency response support facilities, transportation systems and other infrastructure networks should be designed to remain operational. High value manufacturing facilities should be designed to be easily repairable and residential construction should be designed to remain safe to occupy. These changes have led to the emergence of Performance Based Earthquake Engineering design standards that direct development of cost effective and affordable solutions in the design of buildings to predictable performance levels. Nearly $1 trillion dollars is spent each year on the construction of buildings, transportation, and infrastructure systems in the United States. The total value of construction in the nation is about $7.5 trillion dollars. The development of new performance based engineering standards will directly affect the safety and reliability of this extraordinary investment in new and existing construction and the economic viability of the communities affected.

Under the NEHRP, FEMA has been able to leverage a small amount of funding into an impressive series of design guidelines, standards and codes that have spread the experience of a few to engineers nationwide. A recent study and report by the Multihazard Mitigation Council entitled "*Natural Hazard Mitigation Saves: An Independent Study to Assess the Future Savings from Mitigation Activities,*", has concluded the money spent on reducing the risk of natural hazards is a sound investment. On average, a dollar spend by FEMA on hazard mitigation provides the nation about $4 in future benefits. The type of research to be conducted under this program has the potential to greatly increase the benefit.

In spite of all the good activities that have been stimulated and supported by NEHRP, the United States continues to face an earthquake risk that is unacceptably high and growing. FEMA estimates that 45 states and territories are destined to experience earthquake damage. This exposure has been estimated to equal an annualized loss of over $6 billion per year, with a single event loss potential of $100 to $200 billion and tens of thousands of casualties. (FEMA 2001, adjusted to 2004 dollars) NEHRP's ability to expand monitoring, research and the development of tools that will significantly improve the nation's ability to address the problem is limited by the funds that have been appropriated and actually spent on earthquake mitigation. At the present rate of funding, the Earthquake Engineering Research Institute estimates that it will take well over 100 years to reduce the risk to an acceptable level. (EERI, 2003) The NEHRP program needs to be tripled in size and brought under high level, proactive leadership if the nation is to be secured from unacceptable risk within the next 20 years - a reasonable amount of time. The current situation on the gulf coast caused by Hurricane Katrina stands as a sober reminder of the penalties we pay for inaction.

Members of the NEHRP Coalition worked closely with members and staff in both the House and Senate in crafting the five year reauthorization of NEHRP through H.R. 2608, which became P.L. 108-360. We strongly support the results and believe that, when fully carried out, the changes made and funding levels set under the new law will support and stimulate significant new mitigation activities that will result in reduced vulnerability to earthquake hazards and a real and significant reduction in the loss of life and property. It will also result in the savings of hundreds of millions of dollars in Federal disaster relief spending.

Overall, the authorization calls for $181.42 million in funding for NEHRP in FY 2007. The money is divided among four federal agencies. In addition to FEMA, the authorization calls for $12.1 million for the National Institute of Standards and Technology at the Department of Commerce; $61.2 million for the National Science Foundation; and $85.8 million for the U.S. Geological Survey. The NEHRP Coalition will be working with the Appropriations Committee in seeking full NEHRP funding at all agencies.

<u>The President's Request</u>

The Coalition is pleased with the Administration's requested increase of $29.4 million to $233.5 million for readiness, mitigation and recovery and the requested increase of $99 million to $149.9 for the National Predisaster Mitigation program within FEMA.

Once again, the NEHRP Coalition supports the inclusion of a line item in the appropriations to the full funding level contained in the reauthorization for FY 2007 of $22.3 million for NEHRP responsibilities at the Federal Emergency Management Agency (FEMA). This would include $2.2 million for the creation of performance based engineering standards for earthquake preparedness.

Conclusion

The Coalition is ready to work with the Appropriations Committee and the full Congress to support this reorganized and expanded National Earthquake Hazards Reduction Program. For a relatively modest investment, great savings, both in lives and economic loss, can be realized.

Please do not hesitate to contact Martin Hight at 202-789-7843 or mhight@asce.org if we can be of assistance.

Wind Hazard Reduction Coalition

American Association of Wind Engineers ♦ American Council of Engineering Companies ♦ American Institute of Architects ♦ American Public Works Association ♦ American Society of Civil Engineers ♦ Applied Technology Council ♦ Association of State Floodplain Managers ♦ Colorado State University -- Wind Engineering and Fluids Laboratory ♦ Florida International University --International Hurricane Center ♦ International Code Council, Inc. ♦ Louisiana State University – LSU Hurricane Center ♦ Manufactured Housing Association for Regulatory Reform ♦ Manufactured Housing Institute ♦ National Association of Mutual Insurance Companies ♦ National League of Cities ♦ National Fire Protection Association ♦ National Storm Shelter Association ♦ North Carolina State University – College of Physical and Mathematical Sciences ♦ Portland Cement Association ♦ Safe Building Coalition ♦ Saffir Consulting Engineers ♦ Solutia Inc. ♦ Steven Winter Associates, Inc. ♦ Wind Science and Engineering Research Center, Texas Tech University ♦

For More Information:
202/789.7850 (ASCE)
www.windhazards.org

♦♦♦♦♦♦♦

The Wind Hazard Reduction Coalition supports the full funding of the Wind Storm Impact Reduction program created by Public Law 108-360 which focuses on reducing loss of life and property damage through research and education.

Statement Of
Wind Hazards Reduction Coalition
Before the Subcommittee Homeland Security
Committee on Appropriations
U.S. House of Representatives
On the Budget for the
Federal Emergency Management Agency
For the Fiscal Year 2007

In October 2004 the President signed Public Law 108-360 authorizing the creation of the National Windstorm Impact Reduction Program. As recent events on the nation's gulf coast have so vividly illustrated, the nation remains highly vulnerable to major windstorms. We have not yet fully calculated the full the damage inflected by Hurricanes Katrina, Rita and Wilma, but it could well exceed $150 billion.

This vulnerability was recognized by Congress in 2004 when it created the National Windstorm Impact Reduction Program. However, while the program has been authorized for FY 2006 through FY 2008, there has been no appropriation of funds or specific budget request.

The Wind Hazard Reduction Coalition urges full funding for the National Windstorm Impact Reduction Program. For Fiscal Year 2007 the law authorizes $25 million in spending, spread between federal four agencies. The Coalition urges the Congress to support these funding levels. Specifically, for the agency under the jurisdiction of this subcommittee, the law authorizes $9.4 million for the Federal Emergency Management Agency (FEMA)

For agencies under jurisdiction of another Appropriations Subcommittee, the law authorizes $9.4 million for the National Science Foundation (NSF), $4 million for the National Institute of Standards and Technology (NIST) and $2.2 million for the National Oceanic and Atmospheric Administration (NOAA).

This legislation represents seven years of work in which stake holders representing a broad cross-section of interests such as the research, technology transfer, design and construction, and financial communities; materials and systems suppliers; state, county, and local governments; and the insurance industry have participated in crafting this legislation. This bill represents a consensus of all those with an interest in the issue and a desire to see the benefits this legislation will generate.

A recent study and report by the Multihazard Mitigation Council entitled *"Natural Hazard Mitigation Saves: An Independent Study to Assess the Future Savings from*

Mitigation Activities,", has concluded the money spent on reducing the risk of natural hazards is a sound investment. On average, a dollar spend by FEMA on hazard mitigation provides the nation about $4 in future benefits. The type of research to be conducted under this program has the potential to greatly increase this benefit.

The Wind Hazards Reduction Coalition

The Wind Hazard Reduction Coalition represents associations, companies and universities which are committed to the creation and success of the National Windstorm Impact Reduction Program. The Coalition shares the goals of the Program to significantly reduce loss of life and property damage in the years to come. The Coalition includes professional societies, research organizations, industry groups and individual companies with knowledge and experience in dealing with the impact of high winds.

Members of the Wind Hazard Coalition worked closely with members and staff in both the House and Senate in crafting the language contained in H.R. 2608, which became P.L. 108-360. We strongly support the results and believe that, if fully carried out, the new law will result in reduced vulnerability to high winds and will lead to real and significant reduction in the loss of life and property. The United States currently sustains billions of dollars per year in property and economic loss due to windstorms. The Federal government's response to such events is to initiate search and rescue operations, help clear the debris and provide financial assistance for rebuilding. With this legislation, the Federal government can provide increased research funding to mobilize the technical expertise already available to help reduce the significant annual toll in casualties and property damage from windstorms.

Federal Emergency Management Agency

Under the authorization, the FEMA is charged with supporting the development of risk assessment tools and effective mitigation techniques, windstorm-related data collection and analysis, public outreach, information dissemination, and implementation of mitigation measures consistent with the Agency's all-hazards approach. To carry out this function, the Coalition urges Congress to appropriate the $9.4 million authorized for the Federal Emergency Management Agency.

The President's Request

The Coalition is pleased with the Administration's requested increase of $29.4 million to $233.5 million for readiness, mitigation and recovery and the requested increase of $99 million to $149.9 for the National Predisaster Mitigation program.

The Coalition supports inclusion of a line item in the appropriations for the full funding level of $9.4 million for the National Windstorm Impact Reduction Program responsibilities at FEMA.

Conclusion

The Coalition is ready to work with the Administration and Congress to support the new National Windstorm Impact Reduction Program. For a relatively modest investment, great savings, both in lives and economic loss, can be realized.

Please do not hesitate to contact Martin Hight at 202-789-7843 or mhight@asce.org if we can be of assistance.

ASSOCIATION OF STATE FLOODPLAIN MANAGERS, INC.
2809 Fish Hatchery Road, Suite 204, Madison, Wisconsin 53713 www.floods.org
Phone: 608-274-0123 Fax: 608-274-0696 Email: asfpm@floods.org

TESTIMONY

Submitted to the
Subcommittee on Homeland Security
Committee on Appropriations
U.S. House of Representatives

FY 2007 Budget Request

Department of Homeland Security
Federal Emergency Management Agency

March 16, 2006

Submitted by:
Association of State Floodplain Managers, Inc.
Pamela Mayer Pogue, Chair

The Association of State Floodplain Managers (ASFPM) and its 22 State Chapters represent over 9,000 state and local officials and other professionals who are engaged in all aspects of floodplain management and hazard mitigation. This includes floodplain management, mapping, engineering, planning, community development, hydrology, forecasting, emergency response, water resources and insurance. All ASFPM members are concerned with working to reduce our nation's flood-related losses. Our state and local officials are the federal government's partners in implementing flood mitigation and insurance programs and working to achieve effectiveness in meeting our shared objectives. Our state members head offices that are designated by the governors to coordinate the National Flood Insurance Program (NFIP) with their communities, and many others are involved in the administration of and participation in FEMA's disaster mitigation programs. For more information on ASFPM, our website is: http://www.floods.org.

Overall, the Association of State Floodplain Managers is pleased with the budget request for FEMA in FY 2007. We particularly note the essentially full funding of the Map Modernization Initiative and the full funding (by transfer from the Flood Insurance Fund) of the two newly-authorized programs to mitigate severe repetitive flood loss properties. We also are pleased to see the request of $150 million for the Pre-Disaster Mitigation (PDM) program to restore this nationwide, competitive program to a functional level.

FLOOD MITIGATION ASSISTANCE PROGRAM (Sec. 1366)

The budget request includes $31 million (by transfer from the National Flood Insurance Fund) for the regular Flood Mitigation Assistance (FMA) program (Sec. 1366). The Flood Insurance Reform Act of 2004 authorized the transfer for the FMA at $40 million – double the previously authorized annual amount of $20 million. The FMA is intended to support local mitigation planning and mitigation grants to help reduce the drain on the NFIP that is attributed to flood-prone properties that are repetitively flooded or at very high risk of significant damage.

In FY 2006 the Committee provided the full $40 million, noting that this amount was about $12 million over the previous year's request and that the amounts are offset by premium income collections. Apparently FEMA has determined that the authority does not exist to use premium income to support the FMA, and must constrain the amounts transferred to available funds generated by the policy service fee assessed on each flood insurance policy. FEMA's determination is that it has the authority to use premium income only for the two new repetitive loss mitigation programs (Sections 1361A and 1323 of the Flood Insurance Reform Act of 2004). It is this constraint that limited the Administration's request to just $31 million.

►► **ASFPM urges the Committee to provide the authorized $40 million for the Flood Mitigation Assistance Program, and to again clarify that the transfer for FMA may come from fee and/or premium income.**

ASFPM also notes that the Administration unnecessarily constrains the FMA funds to a period of two years. The Flood Insurance Reform Act of 2004 specifically calls for these funds to remain available until expended. Many of the projects undertaken by communities involve careful planning, sensitive work with homeowners, and in some cases, lengthy construction periods (such as may be need for elevating or reconstructing homes, or floodproofing public buildings). Further, if a project comes in under budget, the unused funds should become available for use by other communities.

The original authorization for FMA set per state and per community limitations on the amount of funds that may be provided in a five year period. With the doubling of the amount authorized for FMA, those limitations may constrain some of the states and communities that have active mitigation programs and large numbers of repetitive loss properties. We understand that FEMA has recommended in communication with the authorizing committees that these caps be removed; we endorse this recommendation.

►► **ASFPM urges the Committee to clarify that these funds are to remain available until expended, and that the per state and per community limitations are waived.**

REPETITIVE LOSS MITIGATION: PILOT PROGRAM FOR SEVERE REPETITIVE LOSS PROPERTIES (Sec. 1361A) AND INDIVIDUAL PROPERTY PROGRAM (Sec. 1323)

ASFPM is pleased to see that the budget request includes full funding of Pilot Program for Severe Repetitive Loss Properties (Sec. 1361A) and the Individual Property Program (Sec. 1323). We also very much appreciate the fact that the Committee fully funded these programs in the FY2006 budget. We are hopeful that the regulations for these programs will be ready soon, so that these efforts can get underway. FEMA has estimated that mitigation of the top-tier of repetitive loss properties can improve the stability of the National Flood Insurance Fund over the long-term, by avoiding an average of $200 million per year in claims. A large percentage of repetitive loss properties are located in areas affected by the hurricanes of 2004 and 2005, so the availability of these programs during reconstruction is very important to reduction of future losses.

►► **ASFPM urges the Committee to emphasize to FEMA the importance of issuing regulations and of making the Pilot Program for Severe Repetitive Loss Properties and the Individual Property Program operational as quickly as possible.**

FLOOD MAP MODERNIZATION

ASFPM is pleased that the budget request includes $199 million for continued implementation of FEMA's nationwide, multi-year initiative to modernize and update flood hazard maps. As highlighted last year by the Committee its statements in House Report 109-79, it is critical that the data on the maps be updated, not simply digitize the old data. This remains an important concern because in many areas, old data no longer accurately reflects the risk of flooding. Newly issued advisory flood maps for the Mississippi Gulf Coast are striking evidence of the nature and magnitude of discrepancies that may occur between old data and updated flood hazard information.

►► **ASFPM urges the Committee to again provide the full budget request for the multi-year Map Modernization, and to emphasize the importance of updating the flood hazard data shown on the maps.**

PRE-DISASTER MITIGATION GRANTS

Last year, although the House provided $150 million for the Pre-Disaster Mitigation (PDM) Program, the final appropriation was only $50 million. This nationwide competitive program requires considerable effort on the part of states and communities to identify projects and to put together application packages. When the federal funds are so limited, many of the required cost-share funding arrangements dissolve because insufficient funds in one grant cycle leads to many unfunded projects that must wait until the next cycle. An independent study of the benefits of mitigation, requested Congress, was completed by the National Institute of Building Sciences and recently released by FEMA. The report found an overall benefit-to-cost ratio of 4 to 1 for mitigation investments. For flood mitigation, the benefit-to-cost ratio was found to be even greater, with benefits of $5 for every $1 invested. Clearly these mitigation projects are important in the nation's efforts to reduce future flood losses. We note the Administration identifies an increase of 40 FTE associated with this program; not only will the staffing improve implementation of the program, but it should allow positions that are funded by the National Flood Insurance Program to be more focused on functions that support the NFIP's goals.

Nationwide, interest in mitigation has never been higher. As a result of the Disaster Mitigation Act of 2000, communities throughout the nation have developed local hazard mitigation plans which identify specific mitigation actions. Collectively these plans identified large numbers of mitigation actions – including many that will be supported solely by local funds, as well as many that will be eligible under PDM and other FEMA grant programs. To preserve this interest and momentum, even in areas of the country that have not experienced a recent disaster, FEMA's existing programs should be fully funded.

►► **ASFPM urges the Committee to provide full funding of the Administration's budget request of $150 million for the competitive Pre-Disaster Mitigation Program.**

HAZARD MITIGATION GRANT PROGRAM

The Administration's budget request assumes continuation of the formula-based Hazard Mitigation Grant Program (HMGP) at an amount equivalent to 7.5% of the certain federal expenditures associated with presidentially-declared major disasters. Because of the importance of disaster mitigation and because the post-disaster period presents obvious opportunities for, and interest in, mitigation during recovery, ASFPM recommends returning this program to its previous 15% formula. It is important to note the post-disaster period is when state and local governments are most willing to provide the cost-sharing for mitigation, thus significantly leveraging the federal funds.

STAFF VACANCIES AND DHS REDUCTIONS

ASFPM is aware of a large number of staff positions which have gone unfilled at FEMA's national office, as well as in the FEMA Regional Offices. Secretary Chertoff has directed significant new hiring for disaster response and recovery. We would like to emphasize that there are many staff shortages in permanent positions that guide the National Flood Insurance Program and FEMA's mitigation programs. We suggest that the Committee urge that FEMA fill the available positions expeditiously to better enable it to fulfill all of its missions that are vital to reducing damage and to support state and local officials as they work to manage flood hazard areas and to mitigate the effects of future floods.

ASFPM remains concerned that program-wide reductions imposed by DHS may be inappropriately reducing funds that are paid by 4.7 million NFIP flood insurance policyholders as policy service fees; the fee income is used to support FEMA staff who are working directly for the NFIP and on flood loss reduction efforts, and for other purposes that support the NFIP. The Committee may wish to clarify that the policy service fee income is reserved for its intended purposes.

For information about ASFPM and this testimony, contact Larry Larson, Executive Director, at (608) 274-0123 (asfpm@floods.org) or Merrie Inderfurth, Washington Liaison, at (703) 448-0245 (inderfurth@aol.com).

NFDA

National Flood
Determination Association

House Appropriations Committee
Subcommittee on Homeland Security

Outside Witness Written Testimony

FY 2007 FEMA Budget Request

National Flood Determination Association
Cheryl A. Small, President
9249 S Broadway #200-435
Highlands Ranch, CO 80129

March 16, 2006

The National Flood Determination Association is very much in support of the Administration's request for $199 million for the Map Modernization Initiative.

Flood Determination companies work with lenders in their responsibilities under the National Flood Insurance Program (NFIP) to ensure that mortgage loans for properties in a Standard Flood Hazard Area (SFHA) are accompanied by a flood insurance policy. Lending institutions provide the compliance mechanism for the NFIP and flood determination companies assist in compliance by providing the essential guaranteed determinations as to whether or not a property is in a flood risk area. The National Flood Determination Association (NFDA) is a national nonprofit organization representing both large and small flood determination companies. It has become the voice of the industry and is recognized as such by FEMA, federal regulatory agencies, and lending and insurance industries.

Flood Determination companies are probably the largest users of FEMA's flood maps. We complete some 33,000,000 determinations every year. Additionally, we assist FEMA by fielding a significant percentage of the questions that arise over flood determinations themselves and even questions about the NFIP itself and its coverages and requirements. A survey of our companies reflected that in 2003, we fielded in excess of 1.3 million calls from homeowners, lenders and insurance agents concerning compliance and mapping-related matters. Many of our companies have developed important mapping capabilities of our own, but use the FEMA flood maps, as required by law, for the purposes of the NFIP. We are, therefore, in a particularly good position to comment on the quality of the maps, the age of the data on the maps and the importance of up-to-date data as well as digitization for easier access and updating. It is our belief that each new flood map produced under this program should adequately reflect the current flood risk for a given area.
NFDA has been extremely supportive of the Presidential Initiative to update our nation's flood risk maps. We have appreciated the Administration's recognition of the urgent need to update maps that are too frequently ten to twenty years old. While some older data may still be accurate in areas that have not seen much development, there are many, many areas where a 15 year old map is not capable of identifying present-day flood risk.

We do, however, have some concerns about the implementation of the Initiative. Because of the definition of the effort as a 5 year program and a discovery during program implementation that the needs are significantly greater than originally projected, the program has been forced in the direction of digitization rather than the actual updating of map data. We believe this course of action is partly due to the requirements of the program metrics related to a certain percentage of the population each year receiving "modernized" maps.

Since 2002, NFDA has held technical mapping meetings with FEMA and its mapping contractors. This forum was established as a way for all parties to discuss and resolve technical mapping issues, receive updates on the progress of Map Mod and express any concerns about the progress of the program. We hope that these exchanges have also provided FEMA and their mapping partners with a better understanding of how the determination industry uses the flood maps and how changes in the program can significantly impact lenders, realtors and homebuyers. We are very supportive of a provision in legislation just marked up in the House Financial Services Committee to re-establish the Technical Mapping Advisory Council which was originally established in the National Flood Insurance Reform Act of 1994 for a five year life.

We are concerned about the focus on fulfilling program metrics rather than on adjusting the time and funding needed to produce accurate, digital maps based upon updated topographic base data and updated flood studies. Actual updates require more time and investment and this raises the concern about insufficient analysis being undertaken in order to complete action on maps more quickly. To do justice to the national investment in good flood risk maps, it may be necessary to adjust the quantitative standards by which the program is evaluated.

NFDA applauds FEMA's commitment to producing easier to use and easier to update digital maps and we pledge to continue to work with FEMA to develop truly updated maps as well. We appreciate the Committee's recognition of this issue as expressed in the Committee Report accompanying the FY 2006 Homeland Security Appropriations bill.

We hope the Committee will continue to monitor the quality of map updates while continuing to support the Map Modernization Initiative with full funding.

The following is the Statement of the Village of Wellington by Mayor Thomas M. Wenham. For questions regarding this statement, please contact Dennis Beal at 202-833-5881 or by email at dennis@bealjohnson.com

---

STATEMENT OF THE VILLAGE OF WELLINGTON

SUBMITTED TO THE
APPROPRIATIONS SUBCOMMITTEE ON HOMELAND SECURITY

UNITED STATES HOUSE OF REPRESENTATIVES

BY

Mayor Thomas M. Wenham
14000 Greenbriar Boulevard
Wellington, FL 33414

MARCH 16, 2006

Mr. Chairman and Members of the Subcommittee:

The Village of Wellington, like all of South Florida, suffered immeasurable damage to life and property from recent hurricanes Frances, Jeanne, and Wilma.

Municipal services such as water, telephone, electric, debris removal, etc., were often unavailable and, in some instances, delayed to residents because key Village personnel could not make their way to the Village Hall.

The Village seeks to construct an ***Emergency Operations Center (EOC)***, located on Village property, with sleeping and cooking quarters to house emergency personnel for the period immediately prior to, throughout, and following storm events.

The Emergency Operations Center will assist the Village of Wellington in the following areas:

- **Offering the Village of Wellington employees a place to sleep after working all day clearing debris, assisting in recovery operations, etc.**

During Hurricane Wilma, employees were divided into shifts, with the first shift staying during the storm. More employees would be able to stay during the storm if the building was constructed as there would be more room. This would make recovery operations faster because the Village could send out more teams to clear streets, etc. Many employees were unable to get to work because the streets were not clear. After a storm, power is out, therefore traffic lights and street lights are non-operational, adding to commute time. Employees work from dawn to dusk and they must commute back home in complete darkness.

- **Offering a place for food preparation, storage, and service.**

During the last three hurricanes, the Village was lucky that its Engineering building was not destroyed. The building was used for food preparation and service. However, since it is not rated to withstand 150 mph winds, the Village can not count on it surviving a storm, so no food can be stored in it. There are also no cooking facilities in this building. The new EOC will have a full kitchen and food storage area. This will allow staff to purchase food and store it before a storm and to have a designated area for food preparation and service.

Those to be housed in the facility include all essential Village staff for emergency management functions, such as storm water and roads supervisors and maintenance crews, damage assessment teams, critical IT staff, radio operators, law enforcement, and fire rescue personnel at a minimum.

The estimated construction cost for this proposed two-story 4,000 square foot building is $750,000. Wellington currently seeks $150,000 for initial planning and design of the facility and will seek additional funds for the construction.

Wellington is a 10-year-old municipality in West Palm Beach County. It has 55,000 residents.

Testimony of the American Psychological Association

Submitted for the record

House Appropriations Subcommittee on Homeland Security

Regarding Funding for Fiscal Year 2007

March 16, 2006

Mr. Chairman and members of the Subcommittee, the American Psychological Association (APA) represents 150,000 members and affiliates, and works to advance psychology as a science, a profession, and a means of promoting health and human welfare. Psychologists are involved in a broad spectrum of programs within the jurisdiction of this Subcommittee. For example, psychologists manage the Social and Behavioral Research Program within the Threat Awareness Portfolio of the DHS Science and Technology Directorate. Psychologists also provide expertise as members of the Homeland Security Science and Technology Advisory Committee and the Academe and Policy Research Senior Advisory Committee of the Homeland Security Advisory Council. Psychologists serve as Principle Investigators directing the activities of two of the five University-Based Centers of Excellence and student psychologists are becoming the next generation of Homeland Security experts training under the DHS Scholars and Fellows program.

Overall, APA has been pleased to see the increasing emphasis DHS is placing on behavioral and psychological science within the department. However APA is also concerned about how pending DHS reorganization and proposed budget cuts might undermine long range planning for psychological and behavioral research programs within the department. Finally, DHS must remain ever-mindful that behavioral research necessarily involves systematically collected and analyzed empirical data that cannot be replaced by the well-intentioned but perhaps ill-informed speculation of experts or contractors who lack training in the behavioral sciences.

The Threat Awareness Portfolio was cut 35% from FY05 to FY06. The FY07 budget calls for an additional 6.4% cut over FY06. APA recommends that Congress restore the proposed 6.4% cut and fund the Threat Awareness Portfolio at or above the $43 million FY06 appropriation.

The Threat Awareness Portfolio (TAP) in the Science and Technology (S&T) Directorate of the Department of Homeland Security (DHS) sponsors research to inform, develop, and test tools and methodologies to assess terrorist threats, understand terrorism, and improve national security. There are three broad program areas within TAP, one of which is the Social and Behavioral Research (SBR) Program. The SBR Program sponsors social science and behavioral research to support the missions of DHS and the broader law enforcement and intelligence communities, as well as promote the safety and security of the American public.

SBR Program Description, Strategic Goals, and Areas of Research

The SBR Program was developed with four strategic aims. The program leverages the theories, data, and methods of the social and behavioral sciences to improve the detection, analysis, and understanding of the threats posed by individuals, groups, and radical movements; it supports the assessment of the psychosocial impacts of catastrophic events and the validation of public communications and education programs to increase the American public's all hazards preparedness and response capabilities; it facilitates information exchange across the federal government to enhance the knowledge and coordination of federally sponsored social and behavioral science research related to national security and preparedness; and it develops mechanisms to provide senior policymakers with social and behavioral science theories and data that can inform their decisions. To achieve these aims, the SBR Program supports numerous coordinated activities that incorporate social and behavioral science into coherent, integrated techniques and methodologies. These activities fall within four broad research and development areas that support each of the strategic goals of the SBR Program.

First, the program's activities inform the ability of operational end users (including personnel involved with border and transportation security, customs enforcement, and intelligence analysis), to detect threats and conduct accurate risk assessments. With continued support, these efforts will produce two main products – models of behavioral and linguistic cues that indicate whether an individual is likely engaged in deception or is intent on doing harm; and an integrative model of the ideological, organizational, and contextual factors associated with a group or radical movement's likelihood of engaging in violence.

Second, the program supports coordinating research in public education and communication aimed at increasing the American population's ability to prepare for and respond to natural and man-made catastrophic events and developing quantitative assessments of psychosocial vulnerabilities. With continued support, these efforts will test and evaluate the effects of various theoretically sound messaging and education programs on public all-hazards preparedness and response, as well as develop an index to measure the psychosocial impact of catastrophic events.

Third, the program sponsors activities to improve the coordination of social and behavioral science research related to national security and preparedness by supporting various methods of information sharing across the federal government. With continued support, these efforts will produce integrated symposia and workshops attended by relevant federal partners and a participatory web-based system for sharing information on federally funded social and behavioral science research related to national security and preparedness.

Fourth, the program assembles leading thinkers on the social and behavioral aspects of terrorism and national security to participate in study sessions and web-based dialogue focused on topics of relevance to the SBR Program and DHS as a whole. With continued support, this group will produce white papers and briefings on a range of topics (see appended description of DHS Social and Behavioral Sciences Partnership Program).

I. Improving Risk Assessment by Increasing the Awareness of Threats

To protect the nation effectively, it is essential to improve our ability to assess the potential threats posed by individuals as well as the larger terrorist groups and movements to which they may belong. In FY07, the SBR Program's activities will continue to build upon work completed in FY06 to improve our ability to model whether an individual is intent on doing harm or engaged in deception, as well as improve our ability to model the likelihood that a group will engage in violent activity. Additional work will be sponsored to compare how models based on open source material differ from models developed on classified data.

A. Improving Awareness of Individual Threats – Project Hostile Intent

An ongoing program, Project Hostile Intent aims to detect and model the behavioral cues that indicate an individual's intent to do harm and/or deceive The cues examined in Project Hostile Intent are those that can be assessed remotely and in real time, and the procedures and technologies required to collect these cues are non-invasive and amenable to integration into busy operational contexts. In addition to detecting these cues, this project examines whether this process can be automated through the use of sensors and detection algorithms and, subsequently, integrated with other technologies aimed at identifying individuals who pose threats to the homeland, e.g., biometric tools and databases. The targeted customers of this research are Customs and Border Patrol and Transportation Security Administration personnel.

B. Improving Awareness of Group Threats

Another SBR Program research priority is improving our ability to determine the intentions of various domestic and foreign groups who may pose a threat to the U.S. homeland or U.S. interests abroad. The central activity in this area is the Motivation and Intent (M&I) Project, aimed at developing models to inform analysts' assessments regarding whether a group intends to engage in violent activity to further its goals. In future years, work in this area will be further expanded to incorporate the modeling of radical movements and the violent activity associated with such movements. In addition, several projects will be sponsored to augment the M&I effort by providing additional data or addressing gaps in the current social and behavioral science research. The tools, methodologies, and knowledge developed through this research program will improve the efficiency and accuracy of intelligence analysis by identifying key social and behavioral science variables to consider when assessing the likelihood that a group may intend to act violently.

1. The Motivation and Intent (M&I) Project

In FY05, the SBR Program initiated funding of the M&I Project. This activity draws on social science data and theories to develop analytic models aimed at determining the ideological, organizational, and contextual factors associated with a group's likelihood of engaging in violence. The goal of this on-going effort is to develop an integrated framework that enables analysts to examine the impact of various social and behavioral science variables on a group's intent to engage in violence. The project will model the factors associated with violent activity carried out by both domestic and foreign groups. APA believes that this work could be augmented by research to understand how terrorist organizations reason with respect to target selection (i.e., does target selection depend on circumstances such as differential vulnerability of targets, as opposed to other considerations). Further, it would be helpful to understand how specific tactics are adopted and the considerations that enter into tactic selection.

2. Update and Maintenance of the Global Terrorism Database

The SBR Program has supported the updating of a coded and computerized database comprised of more than 69,000 terrorist incidents recorded worldwide from 1970-1997 as well as the initial coding and inclusion of incidents that have occurred from 1998 to the present. While this worthwhile activity will continue to be supported in FY06 and beyond, APA believes a complementary database of government responses to terrorism would also be helpful as terrorists appear to adapt and counter-adapt based on responses to their actions.

3. Quantitative Analysis of Terrorist Perspectives and Behaviors

The SBR Program also will sponsor activity to incorporate perspective analysis into the M&I Project. This project will involve an analysis of the perspectives of multi-level (individual, group, and subculture) actors in a country or region in which various terrorist groups of interest operate. An underlying conceptual framework will be created informed by social and behavioral scientists and other subject matter experts who are familiar with the region, politics, and actors of interest. The framework will extract patterns in actors' foci and attitudes from various sources of data (e.g., media statements and materials from actors' websites). This activity will add a unique capability as it will allow an analyst to make more informed decisions regarding agents' intentions based on the perspectives of multiple actors in a region of interest.

In addition, a team of social and behavioral scientists will quantify the perspectives of these actors and conduct statistical analyses relating these perspectives to various types of activities (for example, engaging in violence, condoning violence, participation in the political process, etc.). This effort will allow for the testing of social and behavioral science theories drawing on the unique source of data provided by the perspective analyses of various actors. It will also allow for a scientifically rigorous analysis of trends in actors' attitudes and behaviors based on an analysis of actors' perspectives and detailed chronologies of their behaviors. The findings from this project will inform the M&I Program's modeling efforts and allow for the refinement of the conceptual framework that forms the basis for the perspective analysis.

4. Systematic Comparison of Open and Classified Data Sources

The SBR Program will sponsor work that conducts a detailed comparative analysis of open source data and classified data, specifically focused on the information used to identify the motives and intents of actors of interest. This activity will identify the relative strengths of these two types of data and explore what types of information they provide to help an analyst determine the intentions of individuals and groups. The research in this area will provide detailed comparative information on open source and classified data that will better inform decisions regarding whether and/or when to rely on open source data, and the applicability of academic research to intelligence analyses.

II. Improving Risk Assessment and Risk Communication

Research in the social and behavioral sciences can examine how best to help the American population prepare for and respond to natural and man-made catastrophic events, thereby reducing one component of national vulnerability. Public communication and education strategies for natural and man-made catastrophic events are key components of DHS's overall preparedness and response missions, and sponsoring research on the efficacy of these communications is a stated priority of the SBR Program.

However, current risk communications strategies should be informed by decades of existing research which have produced consistent findings regardless of the category of risk under study.

Such research shows that people want the truth, even if it is worrisome and as such, candor in risk communication is critical. People can absorb only a limited amount of new information at a time and as a result risk communications must prioritize and organize critical facts according to the way the target audience naturally thinks. Further, people have an inherent difficulty in understanding certain kinds of information (e.g. that repeated exposure to small risks increases their overall risk) so risk communications must accommodate the known strengths and weaknesses of the target audiences thought processes. Additionally, emotions can cloud people's judgment in predictable ways that interferes with decision making so those charged with communicating risks must do so respectfully in order to facilitate reasoned decision making. Even the most experienced communicators cannot accurately predict how messages will be interpreted on novel topics or with unfamiliar audiences. Thus messages must be systematically evaluated for both intended and unintended reactions before they are disseminated. In emergency planning exercises, people exaggerate their ability to predict others behavior, as a result social and behavioral scientists need to be included in such planning teams to ensure that plans are based upon science rather than intuition. Finally, people generally make sensible and effective decisions if communicators deliver relevant, timely and accurate information.

III. Improving Federal Information Sharing and Collaborative Research Efforts

A priority of the SBR Program is the development of effective methods for information sharing among federal agencies tasked with addressing various aspects of national security and preparedness. Not only will such information sharing increase the effectiveness and the ability of the government to protect U.S. interests at home and abroad, it will also increase collaborative research efforts and reduce unnecessary duplication. The initial effort will consist of workshops focused on issues related to national security and will later expand to the provision of web-based dialogue and interaction to facilitate information exchange.

IV. Providing Policymakers Social and Behavioral Science Information -- The Social and Behavioral Sciences Partnership

The Social and Behavioral Sciences Partnership (Partnership) Program assembles leading thinkers on the social and behavioral aspects of terrorism and national security to participate in study sessions and web-based dialogue focused on topics of relevance to the SBR Program, DHS, and the nation as a whole. It was created to describe the significant roles that social, cultural, economic, and psychological factors play in the threats we face and our counter-threat activities and provide a mechanism for communicating social and behavioral research findings to policymakers. In FY06, at the request of the DHS Policy Directorate, the Partnership will examine the impact of U.S. policies on radicalization in the United States. It will also hold study sessions on topics related to 1) assessing the intent of terrorist groups and 2) determining the long-term impacts of a terrorist attack with improvised nuclear device.

APA recognizes that recent events such as hurricane **Katrina**, as well as forecast events such as a **pandemic flu** outbreak, have forced a realignment of the Department's strategic goals to prioritize the strengthening of public resilience in responding to the diverse threats facing us. That will mean evaluating Departmental investments in terms of their contribution to, among other things, strengthening communities, securing trust in government, providing multi-threat response capabilities and enhancing economic and institutional recovery.

Accomplishing these tasks will require attention to social and behavioral variables in three contexts:

1. Predicting the public's response to various threats (e.g., to what extent will people understand warnings, trust authorities, support one another in the face of threats, rebound from trauma).
2. Understanding the limits to analyses and plans, so that citizens and officials have realistic expectations of the confidence to place in them.
3. Communicating about threats, so that people receive the specific information that they need for effective action, in a credible, comprehensible form.

These issues are relevant to preparation, response, and recovery for all threats. While the Social and Behavioral Sciences Partnership has begun to address these issues, APA believes the Department would benefit from an in-house Center for Translational Social and Behavioral Science Research tasked with ensuring that our homeland security plans are grounded in the best available science.

Although the center should be located in the Science and Technology Directorate, it should provide services to the entire Department. For example, it would be a resource for creating scientifically sound, behaviorally realistic communications, usability standards, risk analyses, and emergency plans. It would also identify fundamental issues, to be studied by the University Centers of Excellence and others.

The Center proposed is similar to the Office of Behavioral and Social Sciences Research at the National Institutes of Health (NIH) which celebrates a ten year anniversary this year and leverages a modest budget to coordinate interdisciplinary and translational behavioral and social science research across the twenty-seven Institutes and Centers of NIH. This initiative would address a significant gap in the Department's science and technology resources, while providing an essential input to implementing the Department's commitment to risk-based decision making.

University Programs – DHS Scholars and Fellows Program.

APA has been very pleased to see how well behavioral and social scientists are represented in the DHS Scholars and Fellows awards. However, we are concerned that cuts to the FY 06 budget and proposed cuts to the FY 07 budget will serve to disrupt a critical career pipeline for the next generation of Homeland Security scientists. If the proposed FY 07 budget is enacted, DHS will cut Scholars and Fellows support by one third. Especially this year, as the Administration and Congress focus on the American Competitiveness Initiative, we strongly recommend that the subcommittee restore full funding of the DHS Scholars and Fellows program.

University Programs were cut 11% from FY05 to FY06. The FY07 budget calls for an additional 16% cut over FY06. APA recommends that Congress restore the proposed 16% cut and fund the University Programs at or above the $62 million FY06 appropriation.

Department of Homeland Security Report Language for FY 2007

Proposed by the American Psychological Association

Science and Technology Directorate

The Committee understands that **terrorists are people and terrorism is behavior**, therefore understanding the importance of the behavioral, psychological and social sciences to countering terrorism and homeland security is paramount. The Committee applauds DHS strong support of a full range of behavioral and social science research.

The Committee recommends DHS implement a **Center for Translational Social and Behavioral Science Research** tasked with ensuring that our homeland security plans are grounded in the best available science. The Committee believes such a center should be a resource for creating scientifically sound, behaviorally realistic communications, usability standards, risk analyses, and emergency plans and should also identify fundamental issues to be studied by the University Centers of Excellence and others.

The Committee appreciates that the **psychological consequences of a manmade and natural disasters** are likely to be widespread and long lasting and that events like hurricanes Katrina and Rita are known to have caused stress and anxiety in Americans of all ages, ethnicities, and disparate geographical locations. Mental health practitioners must be trained to deal with the particular aftermath that such events impose. The Committee encourages DHS to ensure that mental health research, particularly longitudinal research, is focused on how to respond, mitigate and inoculate the populace as effectively as possible.

The Committee also recognizes, however, that the social and behavioral sciences have a much larger role to play than the single domain of mental health. The technological devices and infrastructure that are created in support of counter-terrorism and homeland security efforts will be only as effective as the humans who interact with them. Because many instances of protection against devastating loss since 9/11 involved human alertness to unusual behavior, the Committee recognizes that a significant portion of the most effective defense against domestic attack will be human agents. In addition, the Committee acknowledges that as we devise innovative technological systems to thwart terrorists, the most dangerous terrorist will be one who knows how to modify his or her behavior so as to circumvent these systems. Therefore, the Committee believes that **effective counter-terrorism technologies must be developed in concert with the social and behavioral sciences.**

The Committee encourages DHS to pursue **research on the assessment of the human dimensions (social, cultural, and behavioral) in which networks exist**, such as first-response teams, emergency management teams, communication systems, intelligence networks, terrorist groups, and U.S. government (Federal, State, and local) departments and agencies. Systems analysis and systems engineering are powerful tools for understanding how these networks function. However, the Committee recognizes that these tools will be useful only to the extent those human behavioral variables are appropriately described and incorporated into the analyses.

The Committee is concerned about the utility of the Homeland Security Advisory System and encourages DHS to include an on-going evaluation of its effectiveness. The Committee encourages

DHS to support **research on risk assessment and the communication of risk** in order to understand the framework in which the communicator operates as well as the knowledge base and competence of the audience. The Committee recognizes that an effective and meaningful alert system involves knowing how to articulate the goals of the communication including whether to inform only, or to inform and change behavior.

The Committee encourages further development of **animal models for the assessment of chemical, radiological and biological agents** that might be used as weapons of attack and the pharmacological countermeasures required to neutralize or reverse their effects. The Committee recognizes that animal models are useful not only as indicators of the apparent physiological responses to such agents, but careful measurement of their behavior (motivation, learning, aggression) can serve as more sensitive indices of both long- and short-term effects of such weapons. Further, the Committee recognizes animals also are potential targets of attack in the agricultural sector, so that longitudinal data on animal behavior can serve as valuable baseline data against which to detect attacks by biological agents that may be either slow- or fast-acting.

The Committee recognizes that **understanding how humans process information is critical to developing new technologies for information gathering and intelligence analysis**. The Committee encourages additional research to ensure that such technologies optimally accommodate the human user. Further, the Committee encourages DHS to support research that applies basic learning algorithms to data-mining systems. Such systems can then become language-independent and analyze text for meaning rather than simply the identification of keywords.

The Committee recognizes the value of robotics in performing dangerous work and in substituting for human surveillance. The Committee encourages DHS to support **research on human-machine interaction to optimize the functions of both the human and machine in this partnership**. The Committee recognizes that it is imperative to understand how best to design robotic systems to interact effectively with their human controllers and partners. The Committee believes that human behavior cannot be perceived as a weak link in this interaction because human cognitive, perceptual and motivational capacities are a given and the machine system must be built to complement the human user.

The Committee recognizes the profound effect that terrorism can have on social systems and encourages DHS to support research **on how attitudes and beliefs about terrorism affect consumer confidence**, population mobility, decisions about child-care, job behaviors, and attitudes towards immigrants, religion, political institutions and leaders. The Committee encourages further research on understanding the short- and long-term effects of stereotyping and marginalization of groups as well as research on hate-crimes and the emergence and maintenance of fundamentalist, extremist, and anti-government groups within the U.S. and outside the U.S.

The Committee recognizes the potential for massive disruption by those who would distribute erroneous or system-destructive information into the Internet, the telecommunications infrastructure, embedded/real-time computing systems, and dedicated computing devices. The Committee recommends DHS support **research to analyze the behavior, motivations and social contexts of known instances of successful "hacking"**. The Committee encourages DHS to research effective safeguards that our consistent with the behaviors of the humans that use these systems.

The Committee recognizes that emergency management, evacuation, and the design of egress systems are operable only to the extent that we know how humans behave in emergency situations. The Committee **encourages research on human behavior under duress** and encourages research on designing emergency systems and infrastructure (operation and communication systems, buildings, roads and tunnels, stadiums) that facilitate the most effective behavior in emergency situations.

The Committee recognizes there is a need to put as much attention into **government responses to terrorism** as into terrorist acts themselves. There are a number of data bases recording particulars of terrorist attacks, but none so far that record government responses (legal, military, political, policing; strategy and tactics) on the same time line as the terrorist attacks. The committee believes this information is critical to track because terrorists appear to adapt and counter-adapt based on responses to their actions.

The Committee recommends that DHS also encourage **research to understand how terrorist organizations reason with respect to target selection** (i.e., does target selection depend on circumstances such as differential vulnerability of targets, as opposed to other considerations). Further, it would be helpful to understand how specific tactics are adopted and the considerations that enter into tactic selection.

The Committee realizes there is a need to understand **how groups move from radical protest or social movement to terrorism and** to examine the **trajectories by which individuals move to terrorism**. Whether an individual joins a protest group or social movement which escalates to the level of terrorism or joins an existing terrorist group, the background and experience and psychology of individuals recruited to terrorism in these two ways may be quite different. Moving to terrorism as a member of a continuing group is more like a slippery slope, whereas moving to terrorism by joining an existing terrorist group is more like making a decision.

The Committee urges DHS to **developing data bases of terrorist rhetoric** for important terrorist groups over time. If terrorists there are rhetorical differences between protest groups that do and do not go on to commit terrorist acts such differences might be useful for directing countermeasure resources. When the rhetoric is not in English, English speaking researchers need the rhetoric translated so that they can apply text analysis tools in seeking rhetorical predictors.

The Committee appreciates the DHS focus on jihadist terrorism but recognizes that it also needs to **prepare for a resurgence of domestic terrorism**. Neo-Nazi, constitutionalist, and white militia violence emerged after the Soviet threat disintegrated; similarly it can be expected that these groups and their violence will reemerge as the threat from Al Qaeda fades. There is a danger in focusing only on jihadist terrorism. The Committee suggest that National surveys with unobtrusive questions (what percent of world's population is white?) could begin to track the popularity of ideas associated with the idea that the U.S. federal government is the enemy.

The Committee notes that thus far, Islamic communities in Europe have been more involved in jihadist violence than Islamic communities in the U.S. The Committee urges DHS to continue to research the **determinants of support for violence among diasporas** and develop theories of diaspora experience in relation to home country politics and especially support for violence in relation to home country politics

The Committee understands that Al Qaeda is less an organization than a brand name or sympathy group with many local franchises now. The anarchist movement of the late 1800s and early 1900s had a similar quality, and due to the international nature of the anarchist threat governments leaders reached unprecedented cooperative agreements in trying to suppress the anarchists. The Committee recommends that DHS conduct a **review of research on anarchist terrorism** at the beginning of the 20th century in an effort to apply lessons learned for suppressing Al Qaeda

The Committee urges DHS to continue research on the **psychology of negative intergroup emotions.** Most analyses of terrorism and terrorist motives makes reference to fear, hate, anger or humiliation but the Committee understands there is very little empirical research on hate and humiliation. Further while there is research on anger and hate it appears to focus on the interpersonal level which may be very different than anger and hate at the intergroup level. The Committee recognizes that episodes like Abu Ghraib highlight the problem in understanding intergroup emotions which are twofold: understanding the relation between interpersonal and intergroup emotions, and understanding in particular intergroup emotions of hate, humiliation, and shame.

The Committee recommends that DHS continue to review **criminology literature and research related to gangs**, especially youth and prison gangs, to better understand how different types of terrorist groups on the basis of recruiting, decision making, and desistence. The Committee believes that through research **comparing terrorist groups that do and do not split,** DHS might learn how to encourage internal conflict and splitting within terrorist organizations. Further, the Committee notes that there are cases, such as the Armenian Secret Army for Liberation of Armenia, and Egyptian Group after Luxor, in which terrorist activity drops quickly from high to low levels. As the dynamics of endings are not necessarily the reverse of the dynamics of beginnings, the Committee believes it should be useful to study such cases to learn how to encourage desistence.

The Committee notes that **terrorists are sometimes but not always seen as representing the group or cause they claim to be fighting for**. Psychological research has emphasized attributions to individual actors with little attention to attributions to groups, and the attributions of interest are moral responsibility more than the usual psychological focus on perceived "causes" of behavior as trait-based or situation-based. The Committee encourages DHS to conduct additional research on attribution theory to better understand how actions of a few are sometimes but not always attributed to the group the individuals come from.

The Committee urges DHS to continue to study **why some groups move from local to international terrorism**. Most terrorism begins in response to local issues, and relatively few groups escalate to international attacks. The Committee believes we need to understand when and how this kind of escalation occurs. The Committee notes that most data bases focus on international terrorist attacks and may discount data about earlier local attacks by the same groups. The Committee believes that by studying local terrorist groups whose actions remained local DHS would have a basis for comparison with local groups that transitioned to international attacks.

U.S. Department of Homeland Security
Washington, DC 20528

Homeland Security

DHS Social & Behavioral Sciences Partnership Program

The Department of Homeland Security's (DHS) Social & Behavioral Sciences Partnership (Partnership) Program acknowledges the significant roles that social, cultural, political, economic and psychological factors play in the threats our Nation faces and in the U.S. Government's counter-threat activities. Sponsored by the Director of the Threat Awareness Portfolio (TAP) in the DHS Science and Technology (S&T) Directorate, the Partnership assembles leading thinkers on the social and behavioral aspects of terrorism and national security to participate in study sessions and an ongoing web-based dialogue focused on topics of relevance to DHS and the nation.

The Partnership, launched in March 2005, has 21 permanent members with backgrounds in psychology, political science, geography, sociology, anthropology, history, and policy and area studies. Individuals with operational backgrounds also are included in the group to help frame the discussion around DHS strategic priorities, and more general U.S. government priorities. The Partnership conducts its work through study sessions held around specific topics of interest.

First Meeting (November 20 – 22, 2005)

DHS/Homeland Security Council All-Hazards National Planning Scenario #1: "Improvised Nuclear Device"

The meeting held on November 20 - 22, 2005, was convened to examine various aspects of a scenario that had been constructed by the Department of Homeland Security and the White House Homeland Security Council.[1] In this scenario, a 10 kT Improvised Nuclear Device (IND) is acquired by a terrorist group and detonated in downtown Washington, D.C. This scenario was one of fifteen all-hazards National Planning Scenarios that is a component of DHS's capabilities-based approach to implementing Homeland Security Presidential Directive 8: *National Preparedness.*

The meeting began with presentations from DHS and interagency personnel that described the scenario planning process, offered more details about the specific IND scenario, and provided unclassified background about the process that led to the scripting of the scenario. Discussion focused on several topics:

(i) A critical analysis of how the adversary was characterized;
(ii) means of deterring such an event;
(iii) effective U.S. response strategies;

---

[1] "The Homeland Security Council has worked with DHS, federal interagency, and state and local homeland security organizations in developing 15 all hazards planning scenarios for use in national, federal, state, and local homeland security preparedness activities. The National Planning Scenarios are designed to serve as a foundation and structure for developing national preparedness standards, from which homeland security capabilities may be measured." DHS Office of Inspector General Review of Top Officials 3 Exercise, OIG 06-07, November 2005 (p. 6). http://www.dhs.gov/interweb/assetlibrary/OIG_06-07_Nov05.pdf

(iv) the need for details on longer-term impacts; and
(v) alternative methodologies (other than scenario-building) for threat assessment and threat and risk communication.

The main points that emerged in the discussion were:

- *Effective probability estimates are made on the basis of a full and nuanced picture of the groups that pose a significant threat.*

- *Much might be learned from adapting the scenarios to the specific local and State contexts and the variance that may be produced.*

- *Engaging focus and stakeholder groups and conducting representative sample surveys regarding what the public knows, believes and feels about such an incident may inform disaster planning.*

- *The scenario does not capture significant long-term impacts, which are likely to be greater than any short-term impacts, thus underestimating the possible consequences of such an attack. Studying longer-term social and political impacts can inform us about how the actions local, State and Federal governmental agencies take might exacerbate or mitigate the impacts of an IND.*

- *Investigation of the potential impacts of innovative deterrence strategies often is informative.*

- *Construction of behaviorally realistic analyses help frame threat and response needs. Although scenarios are posited to facilitate strategy development, bound uncertainty and produce useful insights, most often they are not generated systematically and the process of generation is not transparent (making critical review difficult). They are not easily evaluated or updated by experience , not clearly linked to actions, and are vulnerable to judgmental biases (such as availability heuristics, conjunction fallacies, and confirmation biases).*

Current and Planned Activities

1. February 2006: Six Partnership members participated in an interagency meeting, sponsored by DHS, which focused on the radicalization of various international and domestic populations. The purpose of the meeting was to allow U.S. policymakers to identify questions and issues of concern related to radicalization. A follow-up meeting, where these questions will be addressed by the Partnership members, is planned for summer, 2006.
2. Partnership members will serve as subject matter experts for work in several National Laboratories focused on how to assess and model 'group intent,' drawing on social-behavioral theories and data.
3. Partnership members will serve as subject matter experts on the development of a quantitative index of the psychosocial impacts of terrorist attacks and other extreme events.
4. Partnership members will develop an integrated risk analysis of one kind of threat drawing on both social and behavioral science models and expert scenarios.

Contact Information

For more information on the Partnership Program, please contact Susan Brandon (SBRANDON@mitre.org).

For more information on TAP's Social and Behavioral Research Program, please contact Michelle Keeney (Michelle.Keeney@dhs.gov) or Allison Smith (allison.g.smith@dhs.gov).

March 24, 2006

WITNESSES

INDEX